ADVANCING HIGHER EDUCATION
IN UNCERTAIN TIMES

Academic institutions are changing fast.
And so must the people advancing them.

LARRY D. LAUER
TCU

© 2006 Council for Advancement
   and Support of Education
ISBN 0-89964-403-1
Printed in United States of America

Council for Advancement and Support of Education (CASE) is the
professional organization for advancement professionals at all levels
who work in alumni relations, communications, and development.

CASE offers high-quality training, information resources, and
a wide variety of books and materials for advancement professionals.

For more information on CASE or a copy of our books catalog,
visit our Web site, *www.case.org*, or call (202) 328-5900.

Book design: O₂ Design
Art Director: Angela Carpenter Gildner
Editor: Theodore Fischer
Cover photo: © Image Source

COUNCIL FOR ADVANCEMENT
AND SUPPORT OF EDUCATION
1307 New York Avenue, NW
Suite 1000
Washington, DC 20005-4701
www.case.org

CASE EUROPE
Entrance A, Tavistock House North
Tavistock Square
London WC1H 9HX
United Kingdom

ACKNOWLEDGMENTS

This book is the result of three years of domestic and international travels—conducting operations audits, leading master classes, speaking at conferences, interviewing academic and advancement professionals, and networking with colleagues.

It seems to have become a pattern of my writing projects.

I wrote my first book, *Communication Power: Energizing Your Nonprofit Organization* (Jones & Bartlett, 1997), a guide for executives of nonprofit organizations, after working with many of them over a period of years developing seminar and training materials, and writing articles on organizational communication topics related to their specific needs. Based on my travels and contacts, I concluded that these executives possessed a powerful communication tool that many were not maximizing.

As competition in higher education accelerated over the past decade, I gradually became interested in using the concepts of integrated marketing and strategic communication to meet the challenges many institutions confront. By 2001 I had traveled to many universities and schools, domestic and international, to do much of the same kind of consulting, teaching, and interviewing I had been doing in the nonprofit sector. After writing many articles on topics related to the subject, I pulled the material together into a book, *Competing for Students, Money, and Reputation: Marketing the Academy in the 21st Century* (CASE, 2002).

Well, here we go again. As I continued to travel and work with educational institutions, expanding communication and activities at some of the same institutions and adding many others, it was becoming increasingly apparent that higher education was changing dramatically, and that these changes were bound to change the nature of advancement work. Indeed, external factors were creating turmoil. In light of new government priorities, higher education would have to rethink the fundamental ways it raised revenue, from fund raising to student tuition and charges. It also became increasingly clear that the advancement profession was going to be hit hard by all this, and that the pattern of our work would have to change. The bad news is that change is always difficult. The good news is that advancement is likely to move to center stage in the leadership and management of academic institutions.

This book then is a reflection of what I have gathered over the past three years from colleagues, both domestic and international, about how higher education is changing and how that change will affect the advancement profession. Another major theme derives from a conviction I have formed based on hours and hours of on-campus interviews with everyone from the president to academic deans to student affairs administrators to athletics staff to business and human resources professionals to the advancement-team members them-selves. My conviction is that marketing and communication have already moved to the forefront of the advancement profession, introducing a type of strategic thinking that will affect overall strategic planning approaches as institutions expand and alter fundamental practices in alumni relations and fund raising.

I would like to re-thank some of the people who have contributed to my thinking and thank some new ones for the first time. Of course, the points of view put forth in this book are all my own, so none of them needs to take the blame. However, the stimulating dialogues, the problem-solving and planning sessions, were catalysts for developing and shaping my perspective.

Let me first thank Howard Lipman and Terry Witherell of Florida International University. These two innovative thinkers—Howard in overall advancement, Terry in the marketing and communication issues—gave me the long-term association with a major large public institution I needed to develop and fine-tune many ideas. Also, Susan Mesheau of the University of New Brunswick, Canada, took many of the ideas and, together with her president, made their institution a true integrated-marketing success story.

President John Hitt and Vice President Tom Huddleston of the University of Central Florida are in the process of bringing admissions, together with marketing (including athletics marketing) and communications, closer to the overall advancement operation. This kind of innovative thinking about structure and relationships will lead the way for other institutions that desire to become more strategic and effective. It is a privilege to be a part of that process.

Tina Roberts of the University of Waterloo has been the champion of a very interesting conversation among administrators and academic leaders about fine-tuning the identity (brand) of an institution that is often rated the best in Canada. Why would the best be concerned about its identity? Well, the changes identified in this book will over time affect top-tier institutions too, and the University of Waterloo will be positioned to stay ahead.

I would like to acknowledge the rich satisfaction of working with my colleague and associate Kelli Horst on a project at Ferris State University in Michigan. We took an intense look at issues related to the high potential of large regional public universities in a changing marketplace. And we both treasure the knowledge we gained in working with the Ferris State president and advancement staff. Cassie McVeety and Jeanie-Marie Price of Portland State University gave me access to a wide range of academic and administrative staff with whom I discussed issues related to change, as did Gene Sands of Louisiana State University.

I also would like to thank Bill Walker of Dartmouth College, Scott Nichols of Harvard Law School, Barbara Petura of Washington State University, Karin George of Washburn and McGoldrick (formerly of Smith College), Patricia VandenBerg of Mount Holyoke College, Susan Bloch-Nevitte of the Art Gallery of Ontario (formerly University of Toronto), John Fritz of the University of Maryland, Baltimore County, Tom Hayes of Xavier University, Shane Shanks of Kansas State University, Kent Rollins of the University of Arizona, Peter Slee of Northumbria University in the United Kingdom, Ian Edwards of INSEAD in France, Roberto Sanchez-Mejorada of Universidad Anahuac in Mexico, Juan Carlos Grez Bauza of Universidad Mayor in Chile, Cindy Davies of Southwestern University, Christine Babick Saqui of the University of Notre Dame, Greg Carroll of Furman University, Kate Spencer of American University, Kristen Creighton of Carnegie Communications, Christopher Simpson of Simpson Communications, Bob Johnson of Hawkeye Communications, and

Tom Grabau of Bentz Whaley Flessner: All provided stimulating forums and discussions that challenged my thinking and sparked new ideas.

Kelli Horst, mentioned above, was a colleague at Texas Christian University (TCU) who now works with me on special projects at other universities. At TCU she helped to develop the ideas that eventually became the material for my first book. My work with her has been rewarding indeed. She is a first-rate professional with great insight into organizations and their management, and she now is a skilled consultant in this field.

Indeed, my colleagues at TCU have endured endless encounters of all kinds as I developed my ideas. Most especially, I acknowledge the defining role played by one of the most creative marketing and communication teams in the business—led by directors Tracy Syler-Jones, Nancy Bartosek, Margaret Kelly, Gorland Mar, Ben Alexander, Dee Dodson, David Murph, and Victor Neil. And my executive assistant Nancy Styles helped me with the manuscript and with everything else. She has my sincere gratitude.

Also, I wish to mention recently retired advancement guru Bronson Davis, one of the most knowledgeable people in all of advancement. Bronson provided unwavering support and invaluable advice. Also, my colleague Ann Louden, the other most knowledgeable person I know in this field. And my thanks go to Kristi Hoban, a true leader in alumni relations who has explored with me all the ideas that relate to the future of that endeavor.

I must also mention my colleagues on the TCU leadership cabinet: Chancellor Victor Boschini and vice chancellors Nowell Donovan, Don Mills, and Carol Campbell (currently at Arizona State). Of course, all the academic deans deserve the same appreciation. Ray Brown, TCU dean of admission, and Sandra Ware, former TCU dean of admission (currently with the Terri Lotti and Associates search firm), have provided invaluable counsel in many ways, as has former TCU chancellor Michael Ferrari (currently with the EFL Associates search firm).

Additionally, I want to acknowledge President Emerita Rita Bornstein and Vice President Cynthia Wood of Rollins College for giving me access to extremely stimulating and creative people. And thanks to Kurt Thiede at Bucknell University, a leader who offers his institution some very creative thinking. Also, my thanks go to Chato Hazelbaker, formerly of Montana State University, who involved me in enlightening discussions related to state cutbacks and their impact on advancement.

Additional insights were provided by visitors and visiting delegations to my operation at TCU from the University of Strathclyde in Scotland, the Budapest Business School in Hungary, and the University of Santiago in Chile. My visits to the Aarhus School of Business in Denmark, INSEAD in France, Durham University in England, and, in Australia, the University of Sydney, University of Western Sydney, and Macquarie University were enlightening. I thank Fran Flavel, well-traveled expert on marketing international higher education, for organizing my Australian adventure and providing so many rich opportunities to learn.

The many conferences at which I have had the opportunity to be a presenter, from keynote speaker to discussion leader, have given me an invaluable perspective. These range from CASE District conferences, the American Marketing Association Annual Symposium, the American Association of Collegiate Schools of Business, and the University of Texas system conference to conferences and master classes in Canada, the United Kingdom, Mexico, and Australia.

Participation on the American Council on Education (ACE) project to raise public awareness of the stresses on American higher education imposed by government cutbacks and other competitive realities has been of invaluable help. My thanks to Jane Wellman, consultant to the project; Stanley Ikenberry, former president of the University of Illinois system and ACE; and Robert Durkee, vice president of public affairs at Princeton University, for giving me this opportunity.

Finally, the wonderful creative staff at CASE and its president John Lippincott deserve a lot of credit for nurturing and supporting my futuristic thinking. CASE now has a group of professionals who understand that not only are they leading the largest education association in the world, but they are leading the one that will be called upon more than any other to pilot us through the turmoil and meet the challenges of dramatic change.

Because you may regard some of the ideas you encounter as a bit controversial, it is important to state again that these ideas are my own. While shaped by the experiences provided by my colleagues, they are not necessarily ideas with which all my colleagues agree. Many will agree, but some may not. But that's the nature and beauty of the academy. And that's the enterprise we have dedicated our lives to advance.

This is a book about swift and possibly fundamental changes coming in one of the world's most important industries—colleges, universities, and schools. More specifically, it is about the impact of these changes on the people who will deal with the consequences.

After visiting campuses of all sizes and shapes, speaking to conferences, leading seminars, and teaching classes all over the United States and the world, I find it difficult not to sense the onset of incredible unexpected change. There is a different attitude toward the role of governments, who should support education, the responsibilities of students and parents, higher education as a competitive industry, and even the declining reputation of American institutions. Some would say it is an industry at risk. At minimum, it is an industry about to change—and change dramatically worldwide.

ABOUT THE OBSERVER
After publishing *Competing for Students, Money and Reputation:*

Marketing the Academy in the 21st Century in 2002, I was able to see even more of this industry than I had before. All at the same time, I occupied the unique role of practitioner, teacher, and writer.

Admittedly, I have always been "outside the box"—usually so far outside the box that I was standing on the sidelines. Many saw me as an industry maverick. In some ways I liked it; in other ways it scared me to death. I first considered teaching because I needed the money. After I graduated from American University in 1964 and became a graduate student in communication there, I also became the program director at the educational radio station on campus, WAMU-FM. In those days, working in educational broadcasting (not yet called "public broadcasting") could not support a newly married couple. I fell in love with teaching media studies but chose producing programs over research, and I never really completed all of the appropriate academic requirements.

Then, after telling everyone I would never go into administration, I went into administration, where my bluff was called after I complained that our continuing-education program was not what it should be. Suddenly, without the usual academic experience and background, I was head of one of the institution's major academic areas. But because I was determined to continue to do a solid job of teaching students, go on writing and producing radio and television, and eventually write articles about communication for professional journals, I became an assistant professor and earned permanent tenure.

In doing all this, I learned about marketing institutions. Over time, my academic and writing interests evolved from media studies to organizational communications, and, finally, to marketing the academy. Today, I sometimes surprise myself when, sitting in a meeting, I wonder, "Am I more vice chancellor or scholar, more doer or observer?" Because most of the time I am all these at once, I have the rare opportunity to advance the academy as a professional while I observe and write about what is happening to it.

Never before have I felt so strongly that I am in the right place at the right time. I usually felt I offered the alternative point of view. As a graduate student, before anyone else understood him, I became interested in Marshall McLuhan and his ideas about how new media change the way things work. In continuing education, I always seemed to be thinking on the edge about possibilities such as offering academic credit for life experience and giving individuals more flexibility in designing degree programs. And when I began to use the word "marketing" in association with the academy, most felt it sounded like selling and commercialization and rejected it outright.

But now more academic leaders who plan institutional futures understand that marketing is only commercial if you make it so, and that it is really a way to define and develop your best assets as distinctive competitive advantages. And that is what will be necessary if we all take more individual responsibility for advancing our institutions. And we will.

NEW CHALLENGES FOR HIGHER EDUCATION AND ADVANCEMENT

Most people agree that academic institutions are essential to the success of their individual careers. When pressed, they also recognize the role of academia in improving overall quality of life. And most acknowledge that these institutions must be called upon to produce the resourceful and learned leaders who will solve the problems of a world in turmoil—a world terrorized by religious extremists, polarized political interests, and brutal autocrats.

But political leaders responsible for dealing with these conflicts are the very people who are cutting back support for the industry that must ultimately find solutions to these problems. It is a terrible irony, but it is reality nonetheless.

How will higher education survive these cutbacks? Who will solve the industry's problems? And how will this alter the world marketplace of higher education? These questions are addressed in this book, which ultimately focuses on the academy's advancement professionals—people now called upon to raise much more money, mobilize all their alumni, communicate more effectively what "higher" education is all about, and recruit more competitively for the talented and imaginative students who will save our world. Indeed, the whole idea of institutional marketing in its best and most comprehensive form will come solidly into its own.

Actually, institutional marketing is a way of thinking, not a way of commercializing. It is a way to involve leadership in analytical processes that position an institution for managing change. It is a way to deal simultaneously with curriculum, program delivery, and pricing and communication, and to do it while remaining cognizant of the changing needs of society. To this end, the more sophisticated aspects of marketing will influence both institutional strategic planning and future tactics for building donor loyalty, active alumni involvement, and effective communication.

For the advancement profession, this is both good news and bad news. It is bad news in the sense that these problems will be extremely difficult to solve. Donors are called upon to support every important cause that comes along, alumni have other interests competing for their time, and communication breaks down more than it succeeds. But it is good news because the profession will be thrust out front and given a new prominence and a critically important opportunity to lead. The search will be on for those who can face this challenge and step up to the task.

I would like to thank the many people I have met in my travels. Those who engaged me to audit their advancement operations provided valuable opportunities to interact with the people who do the work on a day-to-day basis. In-depth interviews with presidents, provosts, academic deans, student affairs professionals, admissions counselors, alumni, donors, trustees, students, and other staff members were invaluable to shaping the perspective of this book. But I have also included the perspectives of those who write the words, design the materials, and plan the special events. All feel the coming of change. All feel apprehensive about it. But most contend that it will be better to lead change than to resist it.

Conversation with those who do the work has made embracing change one of my primary messages. We all tend to say, "We don't do it that way," or, "This has worked here for years." While it sometimes seems that experience does not account for enough, in truth it counts for a lot. But experience should teach how to adapt to change, not to resist it. After all, because it is the world that changes and demands change from us, we must use our experience to lead others to meet the challenge.

Who finds this exciting? Who can step up to the challenge? Where do we find the necessary talent, and when we find it, how do we cultivate it? These are critical questions at all levels of university leadership and management. We will need presidents who can envision, inspire, and market the institution. We will need the same in academic programs, student affairs, business, human resources, and everywhere else. And we will especially need it in advancement. Front-and-center is a difficult place to stand, and yet there is no escape. That is where we must be. The challenge must be met. We cannot fail. Are you ready?

ABOUT THIS BOOK

The first chapter examines the influence of global changes—from the world at war to still another communications revolution—on advancement work.

Chapter 2 looks at the type of leadership that will make institutions thrive in a world filled with both hostile conflicts and incessant, aggressive market competition.

Chapter 3 discusses how all this influences strategic planning, exploring whether institutions need both strategic plans and marketing plans.

Chapter 4 outlines the latest approaches to communicating the institution, addressing the assertion that mass media is dead and examining ways to organize more intensive activities.

Chapter 5 explains why so many institutions take brand development so seriously and describes ways to do it successfully in a diverse enterprise like an academic institution.

Getting organized for marketing means "integrating" processes in an institution that is more like a small city than a corporation; Chapter 6 explores ways to integrate operations located in different reporting divisions.

Chapter 7 addresses how interest will increase in internal communication and marketing, arguing that internal communication becomes external communication and that no one communicates more effectively than employees, faculty, and students who tell the right story in the right way.

All rests on knowing our audiences well, and academic institutions still are delinquent when it comes to performing market research. That said, some institutions have developed effective approaches that others can use. Chapter 8 discusses the role of research in the future of academic advancement.

Chapter 9 focuses on changes in student recruiting—the increase of one-on-one marketing and the way technology alters the behavior of new generations of students.

Chapter 10 outlines changes in alumni relations—how it will become part of the institution's entire marketing program and try to reach everyone.

Chapter 11 focuses on the new problems confronting philanthropy, from the large number of concerns now competing for the money to real and imagined "donor fatigue."

Chapter 12 is about confronting change head-on.

Academic institutions are much like small cities: Politics is part of the process. Dealing with institutional politics to get things done is the subject of Chapter 13.

The organization of higher education advancement is changing as well. The profession used to insist that the best way to organize was to place fund raising, alumni relations, and communications under an advancement umbrella. Chapter 14 looks at the way competitive enrollment and fund-raising realities, organizational management cultures, other urgent demands, and even presidential preferences have motivated institutions to organize advancement, admissions, and other units in creative ways that best address their most urgent concerns.

Chapter 15 describes the role of athletics in the changing academy.

Chapter 16 examines professional development for the new breed of advancement staff—including ways to encourage institutions to think differently.

And Chapter 17 pulls together some final thoughts.

FINAL INTRODUCTORY THOUGHTS

Along with changing rapidly in ways that force practitioners to plan and lead institutions into the future, the advancement field also is becoming increasingly international. Institutions worldwide are taking new and aggressive interest in fund raising, alumni relations, student recruiting, and communications.

Aggressive interest in advancement has motivated institutions worldwide to improve their practices rapidly, so much so that many have come up with ideas that represent major contributions to the field. Gone are the days when professionals from the United States went abroad to teach the basics. Gone are the days when international institutions had just begun to launch alumni and fund-raising programs. Especially in marketing, many international institutions are way out ahead of many U.S. institutions. Suddenly, we are teaching and helping each other, with conferences becoming more international and providing valuable opportunities to exchange information. Conferences also offer advancement professionals opportunities to find new jobs and cultivate contacts for fantastic international friendships. This is where true intellectual and professional growth takes place.

Are you ready? Will you step up? Will you meet the challenge? I bet you will. I hope the rest of this book will help. And I hope to see you out there on the road. Keep in touch, and let me know how you're doing.

CHAPTER 1

EVERYTHING IS CHANGING.
ARE YOU READY?

Advancing educational institutions is a noble profession. What endeavor could be more important? Advancement professionals make secure the incredible institutions that train political and corporate leaders, facilitate understanding of diverse cultures and traditions, elucidate history's critically important lessons, discover new knowledge, and nurture scientific breakthroughs that improve quality of life. Clearly, advancing this kind of institution is of critical importance.

This is especially so in our time. Institutional advancement has never been more important than it is today—nor as important today as it will become tomorrow. As the world dramatically changes, so does higher education. And as higher education struggles to adapt to a whole new world, so must the academic advancement professions. Understanding how and why the advancement professions will change needs to begin, therefore, with understanding what is going on in the world.

A WORLD IN CONFLICT

September 11, 2001, shifted the entire world's landscape. Along with the tragic loss of life, this horrible day announced loud and clear that the United States was as vulnerable to the violent consequences of terror as anyplace else. Indeed, 9/11 has come to symbolize—as strongly as any event in history—just how far the world's many rich cultures are from living in peace and with mutual respect.

Higher education faces an incredible challenge: What else will produce leaders and world citizens who solve the world's problems? One can certainly make a strong case that right now, nothing is more important than higher education.

Here is a list of the world's problem areas: Iraq, Iran, Afghanistan, Israel, Palestine, Pakistan, India, Ukraine, Chechnya, Bosnia, North Korea, Sudan, Colombia, Cuba, Philippines, to name only a few. Whatever happened to the concept of the "global village" where nations understand each other and work together?

When the Cold War between the United States and the Soviet Union ended, many of us in communications-related fields thought that modern technology would bring us all closer. As technology made the world feel smaller, it seemed likely that the television and computers that connected us would automatically increase understanding. In fact, the opposite happened; differences became more pronounced, conflicts more serious, hostilities more intense. Now, instead of two superpower ideologies colliding, hundreds of lesser ideologies are colliding, many of them quite violently. And there seems to be no solution in sight.

UNEXPECTED CONSEQUENCES OF NEW TECHNOLOGY

Those who studied communication in the 1960s read *Understanding Media* and other works by Marshall McLuhan and *The Bias of Communication* by H.A. Innis. These scholars contended that people resemble their dominant medium. When print was the dominant medium, people were more rational because the use of print requires rationality. But when television became dominant, people became more emotional, adopting television's emotion-driven characteristics.

When I worked in television production, I noticed that people preferred dramatic situations to thoughtful ones. They became impatient with detailed information and preferred quick, satisfying conclusions. It seemed to me that a lot of television violence influenced values and behaviors. Indeed, we had created the first "TV child." It happened first in the technologically advanced cultures and then spread all over the world. The last thing television "liked" was dealing with complex issues. As a medium, it preferred creating emotional entertainment to solving world problems.

Reinforced by the nature of mass media, the tendency to polarize everything burgeoned. It didn't work for politicians to discuss gray areas and complex problems. Arguing that solutions usually result from compromise is not good television. Rather, politicians had to be either fiercely for or fiercely against something, see issues as black or white, and turn themselves into either fundamentalist conservatives or flip-flop liberals.

THE NEWS BUSINESS IS NOT HELPING

Few journalists today valiantly resist the tendency toward emotional extremes. But the news demands of cable channels and Internet services, as well as television's persistent preference for the sensational and dramatic, make it more difficult than ever to find out what is really going on in the world.

Sadly, the more information you process, the more confused you are likely to become. Should we have stayed in Vietnam? Did we really know what the situation in Vietnam was at the time? Some days it seemed one way, the next day another. The same holds true for contemporary conflicts. As a young man during the Vietnam era, I had no idea what to think. Should we stay? Should we go? Did we have a just cause, or were we just plain wrong? You know the outcome of that one.

In the final analysis, mass communication has created vast information clutter and sending out more information merely contributes to the clutter. The conventional wisdom that institutions need to communicate more does not hold up. What we need is a better idea of who needs to be influenced, where they are, what they think now, and the best direct and interactive ways to reach them.

Higher education has a really big job ahead. It must learn to understand differing value systems, continue to teach the lessons of history, keep discovering new knowledge, and prepare the leaders who will have to sort it all out. What's more, higher education will have to educate us how communication really works and the real consequences of technology—especially when what actually happens is not borne out by conventional wisdom.

CUTTING BACK

Just when the world needs higher education more than ever, most governments are cutting back their support. This is happening virtually everywhere around the world. The cost of conflict and war, social and human services, and governing in general is forcing political leaders to ask educational institutions to find other sources of support. And this is happening just when the problems these governments face can be solved only by a better-educated populace.

This is happening in the United Kingdom and the rest of Europe, Canada, Australia, and virtually everywhere else in the world. And state-by-state it is happening in the United States. While specifics differ, the general problem and perceived solutions are identical everywhere. Universities must raise more money, generate more from their supporters in every way, and ask students and parents to pay more of the costs.

ENTITLEMENTS ARE OVER

In many countries, such as France, Germany, Sweden and Belgium, education is viewed as a basic entitlement. Citizens pay high life-long taxes and then, if students are qualified, higher education is free or very inexpensive. These countries also usually have an institution that accepts virtually everyone. In these countries, the concept of "paying back" the institution by supporting it financially does not exist. The thinking is that a university education is more than paid for by all those taxes.

There are so many different "prices" in higher education that no one anywhere really knows what an education should cost. What is a fair price? In the United States, financial aid is distributed so freely that virtually everyone feels entitled to some. Because it appears that everyone else is getting it, many who can afford higher education feel they deserve some support. Indeed, to maintain competitive advantage more institutions offer talented students substantial amounts of financial aid.

Everywhere, little by little, the dynamic of student recruiting is changing. Instead of applying and hoping to be accepted, students and parents shop institutions for the best overall deal—in terms of both educational quality and price. No matter how much money they may have, they do not want to pay more than necessary. Looking beyond selectivity in admissions, they view teaching effectiveness, class size, student services, and job placement as critical quality factors.

There has been a lot of talk lately about the vast amounts of wealth that will soon transfer from one generation to another. Some look forward to a significant increase in institutional giving, but others wonder whether new generations will care as much about their institutions as previous ones. Still others are concerned that current donors who are solicited by every nonprofit in the community are just getting tired, a condition often referred to as "donor fatigue." If every government on earth significantly decreases financial support of higher education, and every needy charity increases its solicitation of private support, will there be enough private support available to meet all these needs?

WHERE TO FROM HERE?

Dealing with these issues is going to require extraordinary leadership at every level of higher education. The executive level is going to need leaders driven by a clear vision of what is needed to survive as well as to thrive. This may mean developing a new breed of leaders, people possessed with love of and devotion to the academy who also appreciate the academy's unique characteristics and understand exactly how to compete successfully for money and students in a changing world. These leaders also will have to know how to build the reputation and visibility necessary to succeed.

In addition to executive leadership, our institutions will need people who know how to motivate and lead teams. Being competitive will require mustering all the creativity that an institution can find. People throughout the institution will have to come out of their boxes and work together for the greater good. The silos will have to break down and teams form to advance the whole institution with as much energy as advancing the schools and colleges within it.

SITUATIONAL LEADERSHIP

Academic institutions are complex, more like small cities than corporations. Similarly, highly political leaders of institutions must have the capacity to influence others. Even chief executives have only so much direct power, and it usually applies only to their immediate officers and staff. Beyond that, situations require leadership and people available to lead at every level—at the top but also throughout the institution. The challenge is to clarify these situations as they appear and free the right person to lead when the time is right.

For example, clarifying and expressing institutional identity may involve establishing a center or institute or interdisciplinary program or another initiative to serve as a visible symbol of a specific direction or competitive niche. Entrepreneur programs, leadership institutes, and global centers often become "situations" that require emerging leaders to play significant roles in the institution's future. Many colleges and universities will have to encourage and nurture such leaders.

LEADERSHIP IN ADVANCEMENT

Advancement must stand front-and-center, prepared to lead in important ways. With governments cutting back, there is ever-increasing pressure to raise money and market the institution. No longer can the chief fund-raising officer think only about the next campaign. Nor can communications people think only about the next publication or news story. And alumni directors are going to need to come up with creative ways to mobilize the entire force for greater support and service.

Strategic plans will have to become marketing-oriented plans. This begins with an environmental scan that determines how society is changing and then outlines how programs, pricing, and access to learning will meet changing needs. Marketing, therefore, will assume much greater significance.

While today's institutional changes are mainly motivated by conflict in the world, marketing as a way of thinking is becoming more critical. And while communication technology has helped create this polarized world, it will now have to contribute to the solution.

MARKETING AS A WAY OF THINKING

Marketing and communication have long stood in the background of advancement. Many have viewed communication as a service area tasked with producing publications and distributing press releases. Marketing, where it has existed at all, has been limited to advertising production and promotional activities. But that is already changing, and it is changing dramatically.

Effective marketing requires institutions to identify target audiences, understand them, and communicate with them as directly and interactively as possible. Effective marketing cuts through the emotion and clutter of modern mass communication technology; it is the antidote to the confusion produced by a constant barrage of television images.

Practiced professionally, marketing is capable of transforming and vitalizing entire institutions. Combined with strategic communication, it can enable chief executives to formulate strategies that clarify an institution's natural strengths, establish competitive advantage, provide the research necessary for basing planning decisions on solid information, and gain the visibility essential to building a reputation for quality. Marketing provides expert counsel on developing communications initiatives for specific programs, dealing with sensitive and controversial issues, and managing serious crises.

The last thing we need to do is to "commercialize" the academy. Great universities need not turn into shopping centers advertising specials in the Sunday newspaper each week. Rather, institutional marketing requires institutions to efficiently coordinate all elements of the enterprise so that they meet the needs of people who will pay for its products and services.

When marketing fulfills its potential, it will challenge practitioners in the other areas of advancement to think outside their boxes. How can fund raisers strengthen donor loyalty when so many others court them? After multiple campaigns, to what will donors respond? How can institutions integrate donors more fully into the life of the university without compromising academic integrity?

How can alumni programs get every graduate actively involved in some way with alma mater? Can institutions become self-sustaining through legacy cultivation and recruiting? Can alumni word-of-mouth campaigns enhance visibility and prestige? How can alumni relations better promote the whole concept of lifelong learning and engagement with the institution?

ADVANCEMENT MOVES TO CENTER STAGE

Advancement will become the academy's most important professional activity in the years ahead, and advancement professionals will automatically assume prominent leadership roles. The challenge is to prepare them to handle each task and to step up when called.

That means searching our ranks for those who possess the potential to lead at this level. They need to be big-picture thinkers who love the academy. They need to speak both as academic insiders and as externally skilled professionals passionate about the cause. No matter what their own advancement discipline, they need to see marketing as a way of thinking and be equipped to explain it. Because marketing, without compromising quality or integrity, will meet the needs of a dramatically changing institution and world.

Chapter 2 takes a closer look at the kind of leadership qualities required at all levels. Because these will be heavy-duty assignments, cultivating leadership qualities for the new academy must become a more formal and substantial area of professional development.

DEVELOPING THE LEADERSHIP WE NEED

Leadership has long been a topic of study. Countless books have been written on the subject. Scholars and writers in all disciplines have explored various aspects of leadership over the ages. Leadership has been analyzed in relation to success in business, nonprofit organizations, politics, and almost every other undertaking known to humanity.

The changes being forced on higher education and, consequently, the advancement profession will require extremely capable, out-front, articulate leadership by men and women who possess qualities not always associated with the heads of advanced academic institutions. The list of desired characteristics will get longer and deeper in the years ahead, suggesting that we need to start cultivating a new breed of leaders.

PROFESSIONAL DEVELOPMENT FOR ACADEMIC LEADERSHIP

It is interesting to think about adapting the rich subject matter on leadership both to the particular needs and characteristics of the academy and to those of the advancement disciplines of fund raising, marketing, communications, and alumni relations. I assume that many chancellors, presidents, headmasters, and advancement professionals have read books on leadership. But the challenges of managing and leading academic institutions today are unique in many ways.

What will it take to grasp the enormity of the challenges of a world in turmoil? What must leaders know to deal with the internal and external political issues that beset our institutions? What gives leaders the energy and stamina to shoulder the task and, even more, stay the course? How do leaders comprehend, develop, and reshape the cultural values of an organization dedicated to teaching, research, and service? Where do you find people who possess these qualities? And how do you find enough of them to meet a future need that already exists?

DRIVEN TO MAKE A DIFFERENCE

In my travels, I have met every imaginable type of academic leader—people at the very top of institutions and in every facet of advancement. The leaders who are making the most difference had almost always been "driven" by a compelling inner need to make a difference for as long as they could remember. As children they marched to a different drummer. They were not always the best students. They were not blessed with so-called "photographic memories" that enabled them to regurgitate all the facts, nor did they have the patience to memorize all the homework the night before. Rather, many were the type of gifted young person who, lacking the patience to work at the pace of others, has the most difficulty in institutional settings. They also tended to focus on challenges that interested them.

Many successful leaders mentioned, in one form or another, "hearing an inner voice." "I was always different," one confessed. Another said, "They always pushed me out front. It wasn't that I was asking to lead; I just wound up doing it." And many revealed an unusual need to be both player and observer, sometimes making things happen and other times reporting what they learned when they tried to make things happen.

While leaders who possess this drive abound in business and industry, educational institutions have had far too few of them. Many current academic leaders have risen more quietly through a traditional graduate program, gaining awareness of the importance of fund raising along the way and gradually climbing the institutional job ladder. They progress because they personify the academic side of the enterprise.

In the case of advancement, some practitioners have academic roots, while others have every imaginable kind of background—from the YMCA to banking. While practitioners with either type of background may become dedicated to the education cause, others remain mostly professional fund raisers, communicators, and association managers. Their drive is to succeed in their jobs, but they may lack an innate, fundamental need to make something wonderful happen. There is a place for these personal-success-oriented people, but successful leaders of advancement in the future will have to possess an additional spark.

ENTREPRENEURIAL IN NATURE

The academy has few entrepreneurs. I assume this is because entrepreneurs are naturally drawn to situations where they can develop unique products and services, and where venture capital and other types of support are available.

To address the concerns of this book, our industry needs to develop many different kinds of educational entrepreneurs. Leaders will need the creative imagination and drive to start up new ventures, formulate new programs, and anticipate needs before they appear to others.

More collegiate business schools are establishing separate programs in entrepreneurial studies; colleges, universities, and schools would make great subjects for them to address. Because the academy will need everything an entrepreneur does in great abundance, our professional development programs will need to add entrepreneurial studies as well.

A PASSION FOR THE BUSINESS

Those who have had the experience of teaching, discovering new knowledge, or creating something spectacular often develop a passion for the academy. Their dedication derives from the first-hand experience of watching others become joyfully aware of their own potential.

But there is a difference between this passion and the kind of passion that drives a complex organization. The latter passion subsists on the former, but it reaches inside and taps the need to make a difference—to search for better ways to harness the energies of an entire organization and aim them toward great collective achievement. Who out there can develop a passion not just for teaching and research but for building this industry? We must find them wherever they are.

Institutions require leaders who love academics and the academic experience, possess inner drive, and have the capacity to build something complex and wonderful. Few are likely to fill the bill. The leaders of tomorrow will probably have strong credentials in one area or the other; they will be academics or dedicated organizational builders. But whatever their backgrounds, leaders must be empathetic to people with the other type of background. We need to find entrepreneurial academics who desire to develop a related set of skills as a part of their preparation for leadership. And we also need to be open to people who are inside advancement now or who currently are employed in museums, arts organizations, government agencies, embassies, human services, or anyplace else where leaders possess a passion to serve and an innate appreciation of academics.

As our list of requirements expands, we will likely have to broaden the base of our leadership search pool at every level. Because people who can address the institutional problems of a world in utter turmoil are rare, we better get busy finding and developing them quickly. Are you one of them?

COMFORTABLE WITH NEW TECHNOLOGY

Institutions in the future will not want technology geeks in top executive positions or leading advancement. Nor will they want people who understand all the latest systems and software. Close advisers can counsel them on these matters. Rather, what we need are leaders who understand how technology has transformed the way the world works.

Along with changing the way we communicate, technology has changed what we know about the world and how we come to know it. As I argued before, the introduction of a new medium may have more dramatic impact than the messages it delivers. One might assume that seeing a war live on television will make people stop fighting. Instead, it has given extremists a new tool for advancing their causes, and it has changed the way virtually everything works, from politics to religion.

One might think that broadcasting news stories constantly, 24 hours-a-day, would keep people informed, but instead it confuses them. Indeed, technology has changed how we communicate, how the economy works, how commerce is conducted, how information is transmitted and received, how data is processed, and even how people think. To position institutions effectively and make the choices necessary to advance them, our leaders will need to understand the dynamics and enormity of this change. Comprehending the bigger picture will spell the difference between success and failure.

In *The World Is Flat* (Farrar, Straus and Giroux, 2005), Thomas L. Friedman describes the incredible globalization that is taking place right under our noses. He explains how technologies and telecommunications industries are converging across the world, how China and India have become a significant part of the supply chain, how economies have been affected by the worldwide growth of a middle class, how oil dominates almost everything, and that it all moves and changes too fast for governments to keep up with.

It is for this rapidly changing world that higher education institutions must produce wise and imaginative leaders, and it is for these institutions to find equally wise and imaginative presidents and advancement professionals. The challenges are enormous.

INSPIRED BY CREATIVE PEOPLE

The most successful people in the corporate world are inspired by creative people. Indeed, creativity is essential to moving institutions ahead, mostly because creativity inspires others.

There is something exciting about creative ideas that are well articulated and realized. They attract other people who feel the excitement. And the most successful leaders surround themselves with creative people and creative things.

Creative things vary from art in the environment to materials that express the institution's competitive advantage in emotionally stimulating ways. Architecture often expresses the creativity of the leaders and the organization. Savvy leaders strive to identify creative people wherever they are, then bring them together in think tanks to incubate new programs and services, or in action groups to launch bold new initiatives and solutions.

Creative leaders push staff out of their "boxes." Along with working in a particular unit, employees are asked to serve on committees and task forces that maximize their collaborative potential. Organizations that do this generate ideas that, communicated with intensity, stand out from the clutter. Creativity is essential and compatible with passion.

WANTS TO BUILD A LEARNING ORGANIZATION

A university is a learning organization—but is it? It certainly is an institution where students and scholars learn. But are those who are responsible for its advancement and security constantly learning the latest ideas about managing, leadership, and advancement?

In my experience, most are not. Few university human resources departments have robust training and development operations. Few managers make reading recommendations or routinely suggest ways employees can stay on top of their field and make use of everything they know.

Leaders who want to create a learning organization desire to get the better idea first. Being first with an idea creates a competitive advantage, and possessing it has learning implications. Management education, therefore, is more than a good investment; it is an absolute requirement.

Learning organizations confront issues related to personal versus work time. Constant learning blurs the lines between them. Most driven leaders confessed to me that, at first, their families sacrificed a great deal. But they quickly add that they eventually realized they could not sacrifice their families and enjoy continued success. So family time is valued, and vacations are required. And whatever the blend, family and work become a part of one world, a world of ideas based on making a difference. These are not jobs, but causes—and we are looking for potential champions.

A DIFFERENT SET OF QUESTIONS

Most driven leaders are not focused problem-solvers. Interestingly enough, their instincts impel them to launch new ideas and projects and not dwell on existing problems.

Indeed, when executives go through the exercise of identifying problems, brainstorming solutions, and discussing the pros and cons of each solution, it often produces more problems and a negative work environment. But when new ideas are birthed, and people feel owner-ship of them, problems still exist but they seem less important.

Driven leaders often first ask, "What has worked?" Then they probe: "What has most excited the people around here?" And then they determine whether they can make something new out of the elements of past successes. They get people to focus on the positive, and the organization starts to move ahead.

The fundamental question is: What was our founding mission? What factors engendered the need for a new organization? That is the best clue to establishing the original "competitive advantage." Asking what we should do next motivates a discussion based on past success and knowledge and begins to define vision. Successful leaders establish a positive context, which is much more effective than focusing on what has been wrong.

ESTABLISHES A FEELING OF CONNECTION

One of the most effective leaders I worked for in higher education had an incredible ability to make people feel close to him. This was sheer magic because many of them were not, in fact, close.

He always referenced their needs and empathetically knew what they were thinking; and he considered their needs and thoughts when he had to make difficult decisions. The result was that staff people, alumni, members of the community, legislators, media people, and others thought this man represented them. They thought they knew him almost as a friend. And in many ways he was.

Connectivity often can be a state of mind, a way of relating associated with imagined interactivity. The best leaders have a knack for achieving connection by being sensitive to what is going on around them and placing everything possible in a positive context.

Despite all the self-confidence leaders are supposed to—and often do—possess, many most-effective leaders have an I'm-learning-too attitude. They demonstrate confidence by exuding belief in the ultimate success of the enterprise and in their team's ability to produce it. But a counter-quality is a willingness to admit mistakes and occasionally appear vulnerable. While they see the big picture and maintain an overall optimistic tone, they sometimes say, "I don't know" and always admit mistakes. What they do not show is any reluctance to move forward—no matter what.

LISTEN FIRST

There are examples of successful autocratic organizations. There are even successful organizational cultures composed of people who like others to call all the shots for them. Employees like the security of a boss who knows what to do and says so. Most of these are smaller operations; often they are family-run. And I have seen universities that operate successfully with this kind of culture.

But more complex institutions almost always require a more participative approach. Presidents seldom lose their jobs because trustees are the first constituents who become dissatisfied. It usually begins with disgruntled faculty or staff who feel that they have no influence on the decisions that affect them. To inoculate themselves from these kinds of problems, skilled leaders learn to view process as a means to an end and not a waste of time.

Failure too often occurs when the right course of action seems apparent but the person at the top is too impatient to use process to work through the issue.

The best leaders, however, listen first. They do research. They walk around and ask questions. They commission study groups. They appoint task forces. They use action teams based on process to get things done. In practice, these leaders facilitate more than direct. They allow solutions to emerge. And if they do not, they move in with a decisive resolution. The key is to listen first, then take decisive action.

LIKES INSTITUTIONAL POLITICS

In my travels, I run into many people who say, "I hate the politics. I just wish they would let me alone to do my job." But I've observed that the best leaders actually learn to like the politics. At a certain point in their promotion sequence, they took on a job where what they did with their time changed. Others now did most of the work, and their job was to understand the environment, see the big picture, locate talented people, and motivate them to perform.

To do that involves deal-making, sometimes even with the CEO. It means sometimes saying, "I'll help you if you help me." It means going around and building individual support before making a suggestion in a meeting. It means identifying the opinion leaders and working directly with them.

All this is politics, and as I often say to younger staff who claim they hate it, "That's fine. If you mean it, then stick to being the best writer or designer you can be. We need them. But if you want to assume higher responsibility, learn to like the politics." The best leaders do. I am convinced of it.

The best leaders realize that often the most cost-effective way to advance an institution or gain instant visibility is to form the right partnership. Partnering with a major research institute, performing arts organization, museum, or even newspaper, perhaps for a lecture series, can magnify public visibility and impact.

The search for partnerships in higher education now extends to commercial ventures. And it is happening around the world. Universities are building more research parks, establishing relationships with private laboratories, even joining with professional associations to achieve mutual objectives. Alliances that go sour can be destructive, but the right ones accelerate progress in many ways. Eventually, more universities will consider mergers to achieve the same impact.

USES THE POWER OF MISSION, VISION, AND VALUES

Most executives and managers balk at the suggestion of yet another discussion of "mission." To many, it's almost a cliché. But the most successful leaders place a lot of importance on the emotional and forward-moving potential of clarifying mission, vision, and values. I see it over and over in my travels.

When an institution can say it is on a mission, when it can say it was founded to meet a fundamental, specific need, when it can add that it has developed strong and meaningful values associated with the pursuit of its mission and insist what it wants to become is based on that mission and those values, *then* an institution can take off and move rapidly forward with strong morale and few complaints. It all happens when leaders understand that no matter what anybody says, a strong mission, vision, and values work every time.

COMMUNICATES EFFECTIVELY

Effective communication is not just effective speech. Effective communication requires curiosity about people and the drive to make them understand what you mean while you meet their needs.

Effective leaders see the world in terms of specific audiences. They naturally want to know what these audiences are thinking. Their instincts help them convert what should be said into language that connects with each audience. Effective leaders are more inclined to join group discussions than avoid them. Because they view meetings as orchestrated processes, they never schedule them unless they have a process plan in mind. They take the time to listen before speaking and speak concisely, to the point.

Good leaders envision communicating as their primary activity;

spending most of the time out front and onstage goes with the territory. While they may eventually overcome their nervousness, they never allow themselves to become so comfortable that they cease preparing. The best communicators always prepare; they never stand up and ramble. Every appearance must be memorable. It may not be earth-rattling, but what they say must at least seem thoughtful and offer value to the audience.

IS PERSISTENT

Effective leaders are aggressive and do take risks—but the risks are calculated and there are never too many at a time. I have seen top leaders calculate that they could afford only a risk or two at a time. That means they must always be prepared, always do their homework, always project a self-confident, we-can-do-it spirit. But the best leaders guard against the perception of arrogance. Arrogance eventually undermines corporate culture and respect for management—even when the person is right most of the time. Arrogance is not necessary, and it destroys effective communication.

Effective leaders see failure as a part of the process. Following setbacks they say, "See, we learned something." The key is to look as if you know what you're doing, but to allow failure to be a learning experience and part of "calculated" risk-taking.

LOVES MARKETING

Successful leaders promote their causes all the time. They cannot help it. By instinct, that is what they do. If they do not, the organization is likely to plateau, and they will eventually fail.

You do not have to call it marketing, but that's what it is—pure and simple.

It is not commercializing, but rather it is simultaneously thinking about programs and services, their delivery, pricing, and communication. It is being fundamentally concerned about how it all comes together to produce the synergistic effect called success. It is what defines an institution's position among others, and it is what produces its visible identity and reputation.

A passion for the business is really a passion for marketing the business because, when properly defined, marketing is a way of thinking that brings everything together into a whole. Leadership has the responsibility to make that happen.

LEADERSHIP IN ADVANCEMENT

Advancement areas will need leaders with many of the same qualities as institutional leaders. Much planning and goal-setting will be led by the team of top executives, the chief advancement officer, or officers on that team.

But because advancement officers will be front-and-center, dealing with reputation, enrollment, and funding issues straight away, they will be expected to display some of the same characteristics of leadership as the CEO. They will be communicating the entire institution and building relationships with increasingly more important audiences, and they will be dealing with many more sophisticated issues within their own areas.

The qualities and responsibilities of any successful leader—being driven, becoming entrepreneurial, having passion for the business, becoming comfortable with technology, being stimulated by creative people, establishing a learning organization, focusing on the positive, establishing connections, accepting and relishing institutional politics, seeking partnerships, being vulnerable at times, using mission effectively, clarifying values, articulating vision, accepting the role of communicator, being persistent, loving marketing—apply to advancement leadership.

FEAR OF CHANGE

Most people are uneasy about change. The better they are at what they do, the more they want things to remain the same. Afraid they will become obsolete, they insist that the current ways are better. Often, their first response is, "Tell me what I can stop doing before you tell me about taking on something new."

But resisting change is the best way to create a self-fulfilling prophecy of failure. When an institution faces external threats, change is necessary, and those who step up and lead change end up with the most secure jobs. Those who resist either become unhappy and leave on their own or are eventually let go. And none of this has anything to do with competence on the job. It all has to do with the dynamics of change.

The years just ahead offer real opportunities for advancement professionals. We will be needed more than ever to meet the challenge of change. The key is to embrace it, not resist it. And the task is to prepare now. We will have to do things differently, and each of us will receive new opportunities to lead.

CHAPTER 3

THE STRATEGIC PLAN SHOULD BE A MARKETING PLAN

Leading and managing change require careful strategic planning. Leaders must understand how society is changing, how that change affects the organization, and what the organization must do to remain relevant.

Most organizations perform some kind of strategic planning, and many now realize they also need a marketing plan. When organizations are engaged in both kinds of planning, the question quickly arises as to how these processes differ and at what points they merge.

At institutions that do both kinds of planning, the strategic plan is sometimes compiled first, engendering the need for a marketing plan. While this appears to make perfect sense, what often happens is that the marketing plan, which begins with an analysis of the marketplace, ultimately questions assumptions in the strategic plan. In other words, people wonder whether the outcomes of strategic planning will actually position the institution to succeed in a changing world.

Other institutions create marketing plans first and then launch strategic planning projects that virtually ignore them. Materials and activities that shape a particular identity already are aimed at specific marketplace needs and already are being communicated. But internally focused strategic planning projects ultimately formulate goals that have little connection to changing marketplace realities and what the organization is communicating.

Confusion results because effective strategic plans must position the institution to deal effectively with a changing world. The marketplace trend analysis must be done first to plan everything else the university will do. When planning does not proceed in the proper order and is not coordinated holistically, everyone gets confused about the relevance of the plans.

A COMPREHENSIVE MARKETING PLAN WELL DONE

After visiting institutions around the world and establishing a counseling relationship with many, I now believe that a well-formulated marketing plan actually constitutes strategic planning. And if the marketing plan has all necessary elements in place, additional strategic planning is unnecessary. A comprehensive *strategic* marketing plan should contain all the elements necessary to guide an institution into the future.

Remember that we define educational marketing as a way to simultaneously consider program development and delivery, services development and delivery, pricing, and communication in ways that ensure the institution's relevance in a changing society.

Let's first examine why plans, both strategic and marketing, fail. And then we will identify key elements for success.

WHY PLANS FAIL

The biggest complaint about planning I hear is that institutions expend a lot of money and personnel energy over an extensive period of time to produce a detailed plan that now is sitting on a shelf somewhere. No one wants to do *that* again. No one wants to endure a mission-clarification discussion or a SWOT (strengths, weaknesses, opportunities, threats) analysis or all the data-gathering and writing if there is little hope that it will make much difference.

Many suspect that trustees and/or central administration have a hidden agenda—that "they" already know what they want to do before they produce a plan—so why bother. They feel going in that it will be a waste of everybody's time.

Also, circumstances change whereas detailed written plans do not, and some plans quickly seem outdated. It is critically important to structure planning as an ongoing process and to keep written material in a format that can be easily updated. Finally, you must take action based on the plan.

TOO MUCH DETAIL

My operational audits consistently reveal that the real culprit is too much detail. The onset of planning involves gathering a lot of information. When reports are written, there is strong motivation to put all of the information in writing. Goals become action items, which spell out exactly who will do what by when—in precise detail. Thick written reports often produce implementation problems with strategic plans, and excessive detail about individual assignments paralyzes marketing plans. Because individuals have to handle what comes at them on a daily basis, they never get around to implementing the plan's details. Only so much behavior can change at one time, and soon the plan is just ignored.

A detailed marketing plan also can drive creative people nuts. Along with flexibility and time to shape and act on ideas, they need to be able to deal with what comes to them on a daily basis. Experience suggests that the best way to change organizations is to introduce a limited number of goals, skillfully selected because they connect the organization to a changing society and are understood by and tap the emotional passion of everyone involved. Organizations change only when those goals become the passionate focus of leaders at all levels, as well as a critical mass of faculty, students, staff, alumni, and friends.

USE PARTICIPATORY PROCESSES

The best way to structure participation is specific to each institution, closely related to the organization's management style and culture. Some institutions want to involve huge numbers of people, while others prefer a more representative approach, with opinion leaders from each area serving on task forces or committees. In both cases, internal and external stakeholders must be involved. Most find this the only way to obtain the "buy in" necessary to gain support for major new initiatives and to harness the energy necessary for moving ahead.

Several years ago my institution staged a Commission on the Future that involved more than 500 people. Half of the participants were faculty, staff, and students. The other half were opinion leaders from virtually every group with an interest in the university—donors, alumni, businesses, government agencies, arts organizations, and the media. Asked to serve on one of 17 task forces for a year, they were charged with making specific suggestions for taking the institution to a new level of distinction. They were told that not all suggestions could possibly be implemented, but that many would be. They received no definition of "new level"; each task force would have to grapple with that. They also were asked to make their suggestions as concise as possible.

The commission had eight university-wide task forces:
- Undergraduate experience
- Graduate education
- Technology
- Community and strategic alliances
- Global positioning and priorities
- Distinctive programs and new directions
- Alumni relationships
- Role of athletics

Each college and school also had a task force:
- Humanities and social sciences
- Science and technology
- Fine arts
- Communication
- Business
- Education
- Health and human services
- Divinity
- Ranch management

The final results were truly exciting. Because, as predicted, the task forces offered many more suggestions than could be implemented, various groups of faculty, staff, alumni, trustees, and students took the final report and established priorities. Priorities were then divided into three categories:

- can be done with no money
- can be done by reallocating money
- requires fund raising

University executives then set immediate goals, developed a blueprint for action, and began implementation.

The university planned major new facilities and revised core educational requirements. A recent study has revealed that five years later, 75 percent of the suggestions are in some stage of implementation. But the most important outcome was that the process had incorporated the people it would have to rely on for future support, and that these people articulated what they thought was important. In addition, it produced visionary talking points for use by the institutional leadership.

This kind of planning activity is especially effective for institutions that aspire to a leadership role in their region. One task force, for example, noting that the decline in enrollment was in line with a decline in regional population, urged the university to play a role in economic development. The institution could host a future-planning commission to address this situation. Another, citing the institution's strength in career education, suggested that it host a statewide commission on the future of jobs that would raise its visibility and elevate its stature from a regional to a statewide presence.

Five years after the commission, my university is involved in yet another participatory planning process, this one beginning with a review of the Commission on the Future's suggestions and accomplishments. Using a similar representative model, the present commission has fewer committees and fewer people directly serving on them. This time town hall meetings yield total inclusiveness, and an interactive Web site is available for general use. This commission could produce a blueprint for action and talking points for future directions as well.

RELATED PLANNING ACTIVITIES

A strategic/marketing plan is valuable because it sets priorities for the entire institution. The institution's blueprint and talking points express these priorities. However, before it can work, related plans must feed into the process. Schools and colleges need to create academic programs. Student affairs, financial aid, business, and other areas must plan their services. A physical master plan needs to be developed and constantly upgraded. A finance and budgeting plan must be made. And a communication component must be produced as well.

These plans are likely to contain more detail because they must address more complete aspects of entire operations. But the same principle applies: The more detailed and thick the report gets, the less useful it becomes. Be as concise as possible, and seriously consider producing special initiative blueprints and talking points for particular areas.

ESSENTIALS OF THE INSTITUTIONAL PLAN

The overall plan mingles all elements deemed essential for moving the institution forward. Regardless of the form of the other plans, the institutional plan must contain nine key elements:

1. **SWOT analysis.** Focus groups identify SWOT (strengths, weaknesses, opportunities, threats). SWOT analysis launches planning conversations and is used in every aspect of the process.
2. **Mission, values, and vision.** Review and re-state them as briefly and clearly as possible. Mission statements refer to the reasons the institution was founded. Most institutions are established to address an unmet need, and an unmet need is the best indicator of competitive advantage. Values are what people in the institution believe and feel about the way they do their work. As the basis of institutional culture, they provide strong content for the kind of communication that builds an organization. Vision statements should emanate from mission statements but express specifically what the institution desires to become.

   Have a pre-planning group complete this work so commission delegates have the statement in front of them when they begin. Otherwise they might spend most of their time trying to agree on mission and vision. The rules governing participation in overall planning also apply here: The design must be institution-specific, since some cultures have several groups feed their thoughts into a central committee, while others have one representative group (or only a few) do the work.
3. **Environmental scan.** A more formal, research-and-analysis project that usually includes data-gathering, trend analysis, and survey research, the environmental scan clarifies social and market trends that relate specifically to your business. Of interest are demographic trends, enrollment trends, job trends, and generational characteristics. Also of interest are data about past enrollment trends and program growth, as well as the institution's physical and financial potential for further growth. Data about competitors' health and aspirations

also are germane, and information about the level of awareness, attitude, and knowledge of alumni, donors, and opinion leaders about every stakeholder is vitally important. Perform an environmental scan early in the process so the other planners can refer to it.

4. **Academic program plan.** At the institutional level, the plan should articulate strengths, growth areas, and new program objectives. Obviously, planning must identify programs that can be eliminated, as well as programs that are essential to the core educational process but not priorities for growth. However, out of consideration for internal morale, final reports seldom specify eliminations and non-priorities. The process should reveal realities—positive and negative—that are important for individual professional development and planning. Final reports can wisely point out that trends change, new opportunities often appear down the road, and weaker programs may later excel because of the energy and persistence of faculty and staff. Every plan should state that the process is ongoing and that details can change as more is learned. The immediate overall plan, however, should focus on items that directly affect competitive advantage now.

5. **Services plan.** This plan addresses housing trends, food services and eating trends, academic and psychological counseling, medical care, security, job placement, leisure facilities, clubs and activities, and intercollegiate athletics, as well as training in customer service for frontline personnel. The overall plan should focus on goals that directly pertain to competitive advantage. This is a market requirement and critical to moving the institution ahead.

6. **Physical master plan.** Most institutions retain specialized consultants who plan and update their facilities and maintenance needs and are essential for identifying future financial issues. As with academic programs and services, the overall strategic marketing

plan should emphasize physical requirements that directly pertain to competitive advantage.

7. **Financial plan.** The financial plan should take a 10-year look at trends based on past and predicted performance. It should include endowment investments, debt load, and pricing predictions. It must anticipate and account for the financial impact of any physical or program growth—maintenance, construction, renovation, utilities, and personnel. The overall strategic marketing plan would not include much of this detail; but it should mention anticipated growth and key competitive implications.

8. **Institutional goals.** This section summarizes the essential competitive-advantage-reinforcing goals stated in the above sections. There should be few enough so that people can remember them and reinforce with action the themes that shape competitive advantage.

9. **Communication plan.** Communication and specific marketing-action goals derive from the overall institutional goals. Identity (branding) message points are listed, along with branding graphics standards. Special initiatives are listed for each communication/ marketing goal, first by market segment and again by work unit in the marketing and communication division. The communication plan shows how each set of tactics converges on different audiences and their desired synergistic effect. At the same time, the plan will show each work unit which tactics each staff member is responsible for, and when.

INSTITUTIONAL BLUEPRINT, TALKING POINTS

After all the data are collected, understand that they are primarily used for analysis and that all of it need not appear in the overall written plan. If for historical reasons it is deemed essential to prepare a hefty document, the final report should consist of three elements:

- complete version with all narratives and appropriate addenda
- "special initiative" blueprint
- basic talking points

The complete version is the least important of the three to implement and thus should go directly to the library.

A blueprint is a concise outline, usually presented in phrases rather than sentences and paragraphs, that focuses on the initiatives that will make the most difference. Everyone in the institution should have the blueprint close at hand so that they can quickly review it in meetings and at retreats. Keep the "big picture" in front of everyone, so that all are aware of what others are doing to move the institution forward. Make sure all units use the blueprint in this manner.

Talking points enunciate the basic themes and facts that shape and reinforce the institution's competitive advantage; get them on the desks of everyone who speaks for the institution in any capacity. Circulate talking points for widespread use in speeches, meetings, and events. Regardless of the topic of the speech, speakers should include points that clearly describe the institution's competitive advantage—and state them with passion.

Do not specify who does what by when in any official documents. Rather, this is an exercise for each unit to do on its own. Each office work culture is different, and some workers work better in a directive environment. Too many dated expectations can be counterproductive to efficiency. They seem unrealistic in the context of daily routines, and they are too rigid for creative minds.

THINK 'SPECIAL INITIATIVES'

Most people, however, look at "special initiatives" and think, "What must I do by when?" If the plan demonstrates in simple outline form how carefully selected special initiatives move the institution forward, people can usually get excited about doing their part. This is especially true if they are not overwhelmed by constant project deadlines that disrupt their daily workflow.

In the final analysis, if a planning activity gets everyone on the same page with respect to the institution's competitive advantage and makes everyone passionate about the same four or five goals, the plan is a success. The process might be complex, but the final plan should be as simple as possible.

So there you have it. One person's marketing plan is another's strategic plan. If it includes all the elements discussed above, one plan is all you need.

CHAPTER 4

AUDITING AND REVAMPING
MARKETING AND COMMUNICATIONS

For campuses to become more competitive, everyone will have to play a role in marketing the institution. The job is simply becoming too big. More people will have to be on the same page with respect to what constitutes the institution's competitive advantage, and many more will need to persistently cultivate all kinds of supporters. In addition to the advancement professionals hired to do the job, administrators, faculty, and students will need to participate. And the tasks will be wide-ranging, from student recruiting to fund raising to reputation building.

Coaches know that to get the best players, they have to get involved in and often personally handle recruiting. Professionals in the performing arts take charge of recruiting their best students as well. And academics in any discipline who desire the best students need to do the same. Financial aid will no longer be enough. Aid plus direct interactive relationships will be required.

In the past, academics have been involved in fund raising and even alumni relations. But now everyone must be of the mind-set that student recruiting and reputation building require universal word-of-mouth support and more.

No longer can professors say, "I'm hired to teach them; admissions officers are hired to recruit them." While department chairs and deans are undoubtedly consumed with teaching, research, service, and administrative duties, in this aggressively competitive environment, the whole university team must work together to get the job done.

Fund raising, alumni relations, communications, and marketing are organized differently in different institutions now; even more variations and approaches are likely to emerge in the future. Regardless of formal reporting relationships, all staff must see marketing as a way of thinking and work together to "educate" the educators to do the same. All personnel of the institution will have to understand what's expected of them, and an agency-style approach to marketing and communication can be the most effective mechanism for their education.

AGENCY APPROACH

In the past, communications people existed to provide services on demand. If someone needed a news release, they would write one. A brochure? You bet. A video? They can do it. The service most in demand, however, was obtaining positive coverage of the institution in newspapers and on TV.

That situation has changed in most media markets. Too many news outlets and information clutter make it difficult to place most university stories, let alone get them to stand out. News organizations increasingly prefer more entertainment-oriented and controversy-related stories; even stories about universities that do appear seldom reach their intended audiences.

Consequently, many of us think differently about effective communication. We now realize that mass communication is dead, replaced by direct and interactive technology. And this has changed media behavior at home. While young people seldom read any news and watch little TV, they spend more time on computers and more time yet on handheld devices.

To deal with this changing environment, many offices of communications will turn into internal agencies. Staff will function more as account executives. They will go out to each of the institution's schools, colleges, and programs and help them develop comprehensive plans. Thus, there will be an overall communication plan for the institution and individual communication plans for priority programs. Account executives will tie it all together with compatible themes. Where appropriate, programs will maintain individual identities, but communications will adhere to common overall themes and looks. Each plan will target specific markets, with key messages and specific marketing and communication initiatives—often direct and interactive—for each one.

Account executives will coordinate messages and materials with appropriate fund-raising, alumni relations, and admissions officers. With this agency approach, the people in academic areas will begin to view marketing more as a way of thinking than mere promotion. Advancement and admissions simultaneously will meet their needs and move the institution forward. Academic staff also will understand their role in implementing the plan. Advancement professionals will end up doing most of the implementation, but people in the academic schools and departments will do some of the work as well.

For example, marketing and communications and other advancement staff still will produce admissions publications and other documents, handle media relations, design newsletters, assist with advertising, set appointments with donors, help with special alumni programs, and much more. But now members of other departments, faculty and staff, will produce content for e-newsletters, build mailing lists of stakeholders, go on fund-raising calls, organize and attend alumni events, and even build relationships with target "feeder" high schools.

All of this will be orchestrated around an overall initiative to make everybody understand the true nature of marketing and the power of coordinated communication. The office of communications will no longer merely perform work on demand; it will lead the coordinated planning effort.

BEGIN WITH AN AUDIT

The first task is to educate the rest of the academy about the power of an integrated approach to marketing and advancement. A byproduct of the ongoing work of the account executives, the education process will consist of briefings and focus groups. To prepare for this process, institutions first must perform a comprehensive operations audit.

Objectives:
- Ensure professional and institutional understanding of the power of integrated marketing and advancement.
- Explore ways to make maximum use of available talent and resources.
- Stimulate and facilitate constructive participatory planning.

Basic procedures:
1. Ask individual advancement and admissions managers a set of basic questions related to marketing.

2. Have the rest of the staff discuss those questions in small groups.

3. Interview executives and managers in key university units, including the president; vice presidents; deans; key managers in student affairs, financial aid, business office, human resources, information services, and athletics; and selected faculty leaders, etc.

4. Prepare a report that reviews strengths, threats, and opportunities and offers suggestions to improve effectiveness. The report also will explain the integrated marketing concepts behind the suggestions.

5. Use the report as background for devising an action blueprint (as discussed in Chapter 3).

6. Perform an abbreviated update of the audit annually.

7. Offer professional development workshops, retreats, staff meetings, and executive briefings to integrate the results of the audit into operations.

COVER UP TO 25 TOPICS

Mission, Vision, and Values

Audits begin by asking all participants to provide their interpretations of mission, vision, and values, and to say how they would express them for their institution. This enlightening exercise reveals immediately how much staff education will be required. Some institutions have effectively communicated these concepts to staff, while others admittedly lack either useful statements or any consensus understanding of the concepts they do have.

The ideal mission statement for marketing purposes, as stated previously, explains why the institution was founded. The founders usually were driven by a perceived unmet need, which helps clarify how they viewed the institution's niche or position or competitive advantage.

While an ideal vision statement expresses what the institution would like to become, it must be grounded firmly in the mission. It should formulate a clear next step, or big idea, for exceeding original expectations. Problems arise when the vision seems to come out of nowhere and turn the institution into something utterly different from what it has been. The dynamics of organizations require growth and development; they strongly resist transformation. Therefore, attempts to transform institutions are likely to fail. Foundations and traditions are too powerful to overcome.

A values statement can be most helpful in advancing an institution. In the search for unique qualities, clues often are found in collective traditions and beliefs. Clarifying and sustaining these traditions and beliefs strengthen ties and improve morale. Clearly articulated values can motivate the troops to march forward.

Key questions:
- Do we have a mission statement?
- Is it clear and concise enough to be remembered, and does it clarify competitive advantage?
- If not, how can we rewrite it?
- Do we have a clear values statement?
- Does it influence current marketing materials?
- Do we have a vision statement?
- Does it influence marketing materials and what institutional leaders say?

Audits sometimes determine that staff may not know that these statements exist or how to use them. Sometimes staff know they exist but consider them inadequate. Some staff just do not care.

The answers are revealing and instructive. They tell us where we need to start.

BRANDING AND IDENTITY

A strong brand evokes emotional satisfaction. It increases consumer confidence in products and services. When expectations are consistently met, a strong brand defines an institution's competitive advantage.

Key questions:
- Are we making a conscious effort to develop institutional brand identity?
- How has this been done before?
- Are there clear graphics standards?
- Do units cooperate?
- How does brand identity apply to individual schools and programs?

The key challenge: maintaining an institutional brand while allowing sub-units to retain their own identities. I will address this in Chapter 6, but the results of this audit will tell us where to begin.

MARKETING RESEARCH

In the past, institutions performed relatively little marketing research. And they were often disappointed with the results of the research they did. Chapter 8 will make the case for doing more market research and offer suggestions for doing it more effectively, but an audit will establish your baseline.

Key questions:

- What types of market research did we do in the last three years?
- What were the primary lessons learned?
- How did the results change practice?
- What is our most critical research need now?

GOALS AND PLANS

I have already discussed goals and plans in Chapter 3. Obviously, one purpose of the audit will be to inventory what has been done.

Key questions:

- What plans—strategic and marketing—have we prepared in the last five years?
- How much did they influence actual operations?
- Does the institution have a clear set of goals?
- Do the goals of each advancement area directly reflect institutional goals?
- What do we need now?

INTEGRATED MARKETING PROCESS

Integrating anything is the result of a process. Indeed, that is the subject of this book: how to get decentralized silos to share the responsibility for every aspect of institutional advancement work.

Key questions:

- Is an integrating mechanism currently in place?
- Who is championing it?

- Are we making the best use of campus-wide talent and resources?
- What are the barriers to additional cooperation?
- What should we do now?

MARKET SEGMENTATION

Even though most professionals know about market segmentation, many are still mass communicating—that is, sending out more "stuff." One objective of an operation audit is to "teach" everyone what is involved in implementing a market or audience segmentation program and to determine who (if anyone) is actually doing it.

Key questions:
- Is communication currently planned for every audience?
- Which audiences?
- How is it implemented?
- How much still goes to mass outlets?
- How are we reaching opinion leaders and stakeholders?
- How much communication is interactive?
- What should we do?

MEDIA RELATIONS

Most institutions have unrealistic expectations for media placement. News media are fundamentally businesses, and media relations work only when the story you want to place coincides with media business interests. Unless the press release is about a crisis, major controversy, or entertaining human-interest story, media outlets are unlikely to respond. Even so, some stories have appeal (such as major discoveries and medical breakthroughs), and genuine experts can get quoted in trend stories. Consequently, institutions must maintain media relations departments, but they should focus on stories with real placement potential. And media relations departments should anticipate controversy and crises by cultivating relationships with important media players. They also should stop writing press releases about everything that happens.

Audit questions should assess the level of unrealistic expectations about media and overall visibility around the campus, survey academic attitudes about the institution's news operation, and determine what is being done—with an eye toward making improvements where possible and replacing unrealistic expectations with realistic alternatives.

Key questions:
- How are we currently placing stories?
- How many releases do we distribute only because internal people request it?
- How many stories are aggressively marketed because they are reputation-defining opportunities? Or because they are a part of a larger plan?
- Can we refuse to send out stories that will not be seen as news?
- How good are our relationships with reporters and gatekeepers?
- Do we send releases and clips directly to stakeholders?

ISSUES MANAGEMENT/CRISIS COMMUNICATION
The most important objective of media relations is to establish the contacts and relationships institutions need during times of crisis and

controversy. Everyone—advancement professionals as well as those in responsible positions elsewhere in the organization—must be prepared to deal with difficult issues and crises. Being proactive on important issues, perhaps in education or athletics, can have a marketing advantage and gain positive visibility as an overall part of the marketing plan.

For example, an institution might take a proactive stance on integrity in athletics or revitalizing a neighborhood or providing shelter for the homeless or improving urban schools. Or rather than taking a stance, it could host community dialogues on major issues. Standing out front on important issues raises visibility and the perception of the institution as a community leader.

Anticipating both potential trouble areas and opportunities for gaining positive visibility is an important part of the planning process. So is anticipating weather disasters, fires, explosions, terrorist attacks, and other crises.

Key questions:
- Do we regularly perform issue- and crisis-anticipation exercises?
- What crises should we anticipate?
- What is the best way to reach consensus on what the crises might be and who would do what?
- Does everyone understand exactly what he or she is supposed to do?

INTERNAL MARKETING AND COMMUNICATION

While we all agree that internal communication is important, few of us do it well. External demands always seem to consume all our time. But strategic and marketing planning calls attention to the need for and external importance of internal communication and marketing.

Internal communication informs people within the institution about events, individual achievements, programs, benefits, and other matters. It also informs managers and supervisors about issues and decisions that affect them. Taking into account the competitive nature of the higher education industry, internal marketing makes sure everyone understands the institution's competitive advantage, basic message points, values, key symbols, and traditions.

Having internal marketing and communications as an audit topic both acknowledges the need for improvement and gathers information about the status quo.

Key questions:

- What publications, periodicals, and other media are used for internal communication?
- What information or issues are we not addressing or communicating?
- How are we communicating our mission and competitive advantage to faculty, staff, and students?
- Do they have opportunities to participate in discussions of issues that affect them?
- How can we improve internal communication and understanding?

COMMUNITY RELATIONS

Community activities and projects connect institutions to the public. Positive relationships with key constituents leverage into greater visibility, productive partnerships, and increased financial support. More and more institutions now enjoy the practical benefits of strong community initiatives.

Key questions:

- What are we doing in the community now?
- What should we be doing?
- Who should be responsible?
- Is it the responsibility of a particular office, or is it everyone's job?
- What is the best way to organize and improve community relations?

UNDERGRADUATE ADMISSIONS

An undergraduate admissions audit should not evaluate the total admissions operation. Rather, it should explore opportunities for increased involvement and more intense marketing analysis, communication, and relationship building.

Key questions:

- Who beyond the admissions office participates in student recruiting?
- What do they do?
- What is our biggest enrollment concern?
- How can we address it?
- How do we produce our materials?
- How can we improve the process?
- What are the key pieces/communications in our recruiting mix?
- How do we balance academic and nonacademic content?
- What are our marketing targets?
- How do we select new ones?

FUND-RAISING COMMUNICATIONS

Fund-raising communications should reflect the institution's overall branding and graphics standards. Brochures, solicitation letters, invitations, and donor lists all advance understanding and support of a vitally important market segment. But there is disagreement over whether fund-raising campaigns should have their own logos. Much like schools or colleges, fund-raising campaigns may be viewed as sub-brands that carry the branding themes and "look" of the entire institution. Audit questions should determine how institutions *do* communicate as opposed to how they *should* communicate.

Key questions:
- Do materials adhere to the message and graphics standards of the institution?
- Do events reinforce the message?
- What is the best way to accomplish this while fulfilling fund-raising goals?
- Does our campaign have its own logo and look?
- How are our materials—campaign and others—produced?
- How can we improve the process?

PUBLICATIONS PRODUCTION

The two big publications issues are:
- maintaining control over look and content
- improving production efficiency

The publications office is responsible for making sure the institution has a consistent brand identity and that individual units preserve their individual identities. But because publications offices usually have more tasks than resources, they are open to charges that "they take too long and it costs too much."

Producing publications is a complicated process that involves both artistic creativity and logistical management. Most publication office "customers" have no idea how many steps are involved, and, for that matter, really do not care. Customers make naïve assumptions about the status of projects because they have no clue about what it takes to complete them. They often erroneously believe a project is sailing through production even though they have not submitted all necessary information.

Audits establish a starting point for fixing problems.

Key questions:
- Are there clear message and graphics standards?
- Who determines the message and look of publications?
- How can we improve the decision-making process?
- Are our publications of high quality and produced on time?
- How can we improve the production system?

Audits sometimes reveal that academics and others claim publication offices are inefficient to justify taking projects off campus. But conversely, the lack of flexibility within publications offices to work hard to meet client needs contributes to the problem. Audits, follow-up reports, and post-audit discussions will clarify and resolve the situation.

USE OF SPECIAL EVENTS
View special events as strategic communication tools, not merely social occasions. Special events are opportunities to communicate with key people in captive situations.

The audit can make this point and identify areas that need improvement. In the years ahead, special events will become increasingly important. They facilitate interactive communication with key people in controlled situations where strategic messages can be effectively transmitted and important relationships cultivated.

Key questions:
- Should we incorporate brand messages and design into all events?
- What is the process for planning an event, from invitation to evaluation?
- Who participates?
- How can we improve the process?

INSTITUTIONAL AND PROGRAM ADVERTISING

Much advertising is a waste of money. Advertising can be effective. But it is critical to combine careful placement and sufficient saturation with writing and design talent and sufficient funds. Advertising creates presence in strategic locations and functions effectively as a part of multimedia campaigns. Audit questions will determine when and how advertising might be effective for particular institutions.

Key questions:
- Where do we place advertising?
- How do we decide how much to buy?
- What are our advertising objectives?
- How do we evaluate it?
- Do we buy in special sections?
- How do we decide?

- How do we handle sales representatives?
- When and how does planning take place?

Institutional advertising can establish a presence in other locations, but this requires saturation. Carefully orchestrated, it also can work when coordinated with direct mail and other initiatives. Audits sort out these issues as preparation for planning.

WEB-SITE EFFECTIVENESS

Everyone sees an institution's Web site from his or her own vantage point. Some see it as a marketing tool, others as a place for information storage and retrieval, and others as a personal communication device. Most blame others because their departmental or personal site is not better than it is. Most also want their sites to look different from the rest and to control what they see as theirs.

Because it is assumed that their job is to maintain and design or redesign sites on demand, central Web-site professionals are always on the firing line. And because they are coordinating the sites, it always seems that they police the system but are never available to do the work. Because work is always farmed out, what do these guys do?

Audits sort out the issues and lay the groundwork for constructive discussions.

Key questions:
- What are the objectives of the Web site?
- Are we happy with the university's home page?
- Are we happy with ours?
- How does the navigation work?

- Does it have the right features?
- How could we improve the sites?
- How does the construction system work, i.e., design, update, maintenance?
- How could we improve it?

ALUMNI COMMUNICATION

Alumni associations increasingly will be called upon to help with student recruiting and reputation building, as well as with fund raising. They will be asked to help make the institution even more of a lifelong learning resource. Audits need to prepare alumni associations to accept much greater responsibility over time.

Key questions:
- What are the basic tools for communicating with alumni?
- Do we take lifecycle factors into account when planning programs?
- Are we involved with student recruiting? Reputation building? Fund raising? Continuing education?
- Do we work with individual academic departments?
- How do we use Internet technology?
- Do we program for special interests?
- Which special interests?
- Are we involved with overall university planning?
- What are our biggest needs?

ATHLETICS MARKETING

While athletics marketing operates as a separate organization in most institutions, it should be seen as a legitimate and effective visibility and reputation building tool. But athletics marketing must be integrated with university marketing so that each department can see opportunities to promote the other and for overall institutional branding to take place.

Key questions:

- To what extent is athletics marketing separate from the university?
- Does athletics messaging and design adhere to university standards?
- Does university marketing assist athletics?
- Is there a process for ensuring cooperation?

GRADUATE STUDENT MARKETING

Individual academic departments traditionally have been responsible for graduate student recruiting, which usually involves direct personal contact with undergraduate programs. While marketing professionals traditionally have offered little assistance, many graduate program deans are beginning to ask for more help.

Key questions:

- What role do marketing and communication currently play in graduate student recruitment?
- What is the graduate studies office doing?
- What are individual departments doing?
- What materials do we currently produce?
- Who is producing them?
- What are perceived current and future needs?

ADULT STUDENT RECRUITING

Because they have designed and marketed their own programs all along, continuing education professionals are usually the most experienced marketers in the entire institution. They have had to do marketing outside the normal undergraduate admissions operation, often without substantial assistance from the communications office. When institutions decide to intensify their overall marketing operations, they regard continuing adult education as a pool for experienced talent.

Future market competition will motivate institutions to place increased emphasis on lifelong learning. Along with offering more programs that encourage their own students to return for updates and enrichment, institutions will reach out to other adults in their region and beyond with everything from courses and seminars to symposia and in-depth institutes. Learning will take place on campus, online, and around the world. Alumni relations programs and fund raisers will need to get far more involved in marketing, paying more attention to reinforcing both the lifelong learning concept and to devising exciting new programs for alumni and donors of all ages and interests.

Key questions:

- What role does marketing currently play in adult student recruiting?
- What materials currently exist?
- Who produces them?
- To what extent are all areas of advancement involved?
- How can we best approach this to meet future needs?

DEVELOPING OUR HUMAN RESOURCES

The future will require highly prepared leadership at all levels but especially in every area of advancement work. In the past, academic institutions conceded the best marketing talent to other industries, hiring people who were willing to sacrifice income to work in a campus environment. Now, the demands of higher education advancement require highly talented people who are willing to work long hours and eager for opportunities to move up within the industry.

Education is a complex industry. It is challenging to define the products, let alone get everyone headed in the same direction. People outside education may think that our jobs are easy, nothing but long holidays and lazy afternoons strolling the campus. In fact, all areas of advancement require even more talent, dedication, and energy than similar positions elsewhere. Most advancement professionals are either on call over weekends or work weekends as a matter of routine. Many travel, meet endless deadlines, and deal with the academy's political issues as well. When I hire people currently working in business, I quiz them intensely about their work expectations. Afterwards, most concede that when they get into education, their work commitments are likely to become even more intense.

The emotional and professional rewards of advancing education are high, but to attract and retain top talent we will have to increase economic and career rewards and take professional development more seriously.

Key questions:
- Do we have adequate staffing in every area of advancement?
- Where are we deficient?
- What are our compensation issues?

- What will we need to build the internal marketing agency described earlier?
- Do we have the leadership?
- Where can we find it?
- Do we have sufficient talent in each area?

ORGANIZATIONAL STRUCTURE

Many institutions believe restructuring will improve efficiency. The traditional advancement structure that combines fund raising, alumni relations, and marketing/communications still works for some but not for others. (I address this in more detail in Chapter 14.) Audits put the issue on the table and collect ideas about what will improve working relationships and efficiency.

Key questions:
- Does the current structure work effectively for us?
- What would make us more efficient?
- What combination of restructured and integrated processes should we consider?

MANAGEMENT COMMUNICATION

While communicating important information about the organization is the responsibility of management, few managers take that part of their role to heart. Communication departments distribute basic information, but staff seldom act on it unless they hear it directly from a manager or supervisor. Many know about developments but deny it, saying, "They didn't tell me." This is an excuse for not acting that really means, "I didn't hear it from my boss." On the other hand, what they hear on the grapevine does shape their attitudes and motivation and too often turns out to be true. Rumors influence how much respect staff has or does not have for leadership. No matter how effective your internal communication and marketing operation, if management does not communicate directly with staff the entire process fails.

Address management communication policies, expectations, and training as a part of strategic and marketing planning. Getting everyone on the same page means covering everything—from reinforcing identity messages to major initiatives to individual benefits. Managers have to inform staff at the same time the materials are rolling out. The audit is an opportunity to emphasize that management communication is a key part of the process.

Key questions:
- How effective is existing management communication?
- What needs to be improved?
- What is the best way to improve it?
- How can we coordinate it with the rest of marketing and communication?

ACADEMIC ATTITUDES

Assessing current academic attitudes is an essential part of the process. In some institutions, "marketing" is still a dirty word, though this is changing rapidly. In others, fund raising is something someone else does or something done independently by individual programs. Some institutions view alumni relations as mostly fun and games and almost totally tied to athletics; others see it much differently.

It is important to know what people think. It is also important to know what people think other people think. How do academics feel? What impressions do advancement people have? Do not waste time trying to convert the problem people. Instead, mobilize supporters and move ahead. But first find out where everyone stands.

Key questions:
- How do we feel about academic marketing?
- Under what conditions would we support it?
- Who is responsible for fund raising?
- How should we coordinate it?
- What do we think about the alumni relations program?
- How can we improve it?

While some of these questions overlap previous questions, putting them together and asking them in this context emphasizes that these issues will have to be resolved.

EXECUTIVE ATTITUDES

It is essential to know where each executive stands on these issues. The president's support is vital. If the president is ambivalent, the problem becomes more serious. But I have seen presidents authorize integrated programs with great reluctance, only to join in enthusiastically after they get rolling. I also have seen provosts behave the same way. The key is to mobilize the supporters—but you have to find out who they are. If most of the top executives are entirely uninterested, all of this will have to wait for another day.

Dynamic change often takes place during transition periods. New presidents or deans come onboard with enthusiasm for this kind of thinking. But the opposite occurs as well. When new leaders are enthusiastic, programs take off; if not, programs languish for a while. But even then, momentum returns after an initial period of adjustment— if advancement people continue interacting with the true believers.

Key questions:

- How do we assess the institution's reputation and visibility?
- How do we feel about educational marketing?
- Under what conditions would we support it?
- How should we coordinate fund raising?
- What do we expect from alumni relations?
- Are we willing to help get everyone on the same page and then "walk the talk"?

OVERALL ADVANCEMENT TEAM ASSESSMENT

Audit reports should first summarize the current state of the advancement areas and then prescribe actions to meet the challenges ahead. The report should address admissions, athletics, and any other area deemed critical to mobilizing talent and resources.

AUDIT REPORT

Audit reports should address every topic covered in this chapter, describing why each area was analyzed and its role in an integrated program. Reports should point out strengths to nurture, weaknesses to repair, and areas that need improvement.

Reports will become educational documents, introducing the basic concepts of integrated marketing and advancement. They will also set the agenda for constructive discussions that move the institution forward.

But do not assume everyone will read it. Follow up with briefings, discussions, and training. I will describe the most effective integrated processes in the pages ahead.

CHAPTER 5

STRENGTHENING COMPETITIVE ADVANTAGE

M ost comprehensive audits persuade the institution that it should establish a distinct identity, in terms of its competitors, and that as many people as possible, inside and outside the institution, should understand and communicate it.

Today's competitive environment requires institutions to do a better job of explaining what differentiates them and, therefore, what makes them better. It means differentiating themselves within the market-place and gaining a deeper understanding of the competition. And it means clarifying all message points.

Even very large public universities are asking, "Besides being large, comprehensive, research-oriented, and public, what makes us distinctive?" Some have trouble coming up with good answers, but many discover that location, strong programs, and student-body mix may be attractive differentiating factors. The more an institution differentiates itself, the more selective its distinctiveness allows it to become. Sometimes differentiation narrows the potential market, but the narrower the market segment the more national and international its reach. When an institution can claim, based on a set of descriptors, that it is the world's best in a specific area, it has a powerful message.

Top-tier institutions attract the best students with their stature and wealth. That will no doubt remain the case for some time. However, many schools just below the top rung are rethinking their game plans. The "ratings game" is being tested. As every institution struggles to improve its ratings, all gradually rise together. As a result, it is almost impossible to change ratings dramatically. And do consumers really care if an institution moves from number 75 to 71?

More institutions will use their distinctive qualities to redefine their market objectives. The more distinctive an institution, the more credible its claim that it is the best at what it does. *Good to Great: Why Some Companies Make the Leap...and Others Don't*, by Jim Collins (HarperCollins, 2001), explores the difference between good enterprises and great ones. High on list of characteristics of great ones are products that are so distinctive that the companies can confidently claim they are the best in the world.

An example frequently cited from the business world is 7UP®, which, once it realized it was always likely to be second to cola drinks, invented a new industry category: Uncola. In this new category, 7UP® became number one.

Marketing professionals advise against focusing on the "features" of the college experience; they prefer instead to promote individual "benefits." While this is good advice, your features merge into your institutional identity. Clustering of features is the heart of differentiation, the key to distinction.

Even the top universities are going to delineate specific areas where they can claim greatness; as consumers get used to the greater differentiation, the marketplace for the top tier is likely to change as well. One or two institutions already have shown interest in identity clarification. In the introduction, I cited the University of Waterloo in Canada, and there is a glimmer of it in the United States as well.

UNDERSTANDING THE POWER OF BRAND

What I really have been talking about is branding, a word that, like "marketing," is not always embraced by the academy. But that is changing as people understand it better. I have used terms like "identity" and "competitive advantage" and "positioning" to discuss different facets of the same phenomenon. What drives this conversation is increased awareness that consumers are buying a lifetime "brand" association. In a way, it is our primary product.

Some students choose one school over another because of a specific program or its location or an acquaintance already at the school. But weighing heavily in the equation is brand identity. Will I be proud of my connection to the institution? Can I identify with what it stands for? Do I feel good about the experience I anticipate? Brand is a powerful differentiating factor, and more educators realize that shaping brand is a major factor in competitive success.

WHAT A BRAND IS NOT

A brand is not a logo. It is not a single mark or a word in a particular typeface. Neither is brand a particular design or look or color. It is none of these things alone. Rather, it is a set of feelings and impressions about an institution that these design characteristics come to represent. Our challenge is to make that happen in a uniform and consistent way.

A brand is the *essence* of an organization, product, or service that establishes distinction. It is a set of consistent emotions that are elicited when the entity is mentioned. Over time, brand achieves a bond and eventually makes consumers feel better about the entity just because they are familiar with it.

A brand, therefore, is often referred to as a "promise," the promise of a particular kind of experience. But if people do not have that experience, all bets are off. The brand must be connected to reality, and all members of the organization must understand their roles in delivering it. Consistency of product and service is essential, as is clarity and consistency of message.

ROLE OF LOGO AND DESIGN

When a set of consistent message points is associated with a logo and design, together they build the brand. In time, the logo can stand for those message points and promises, but the brand is not the mark itself. It is the particular set of feelings and impressions associated with it.

Building the brand must be a systematic and cooperative process. Because the basic message points must be consistent over time and always associated with similar design features and logos, everyone involved in communication must participate in the brand-building process. The longer the process lasts the stronger the brand becomes.

ROLE OF SUB-BRANDS

In academic institutions, specific schools, colleges, and programs often claim unique identities. These are higher education sub-brands that must be acknowledged and embraced. Business schools must be able to connect with business audiences; the same is true for fine arts, technology, medicine, and every other school.

Building sub-brands means permitting the sub-entity to retain a unique identity within the overall look and logo of the institution. Some institutions have established a ratio: Perhaps 85 percent of the business school's materials can look like business, while 15 percent must look like the overall university's. This can be literally 15 percent of the space across the top or along the side of publications, or it could involve consistent use of lines, colors, and placement of logos.

Some institutions deny sub-brands their own logos. Sub-brands can have unique message points and photos of their facilities but no logo. Others allow sub-brand logos, but they insist that the sub-brand logos resemble the institutional logo and limit its placement.

All this involves creating design standards that are flexible and not too restrictive but establish brand consistency. Within a climate of cooperation, it certainly is possible bring this about.

Audit exercises, as discussed in Chapter 4, set the stage for cooperation. Brief meetings about the results and the audit's implications for change will further the process. An accompanying written report will make a strong case for brand consistency, stressing the importance of an institutional brand identity and outlining how to achieve it without sacrificing individual identities and independence.

Under the internal agency model described in Chapter 4, account executives must assure each dean and program head that they will help them put their individual programs on the map. Deans and program heads must understand that the agency approach will help them cultivate, not eliminate, their program's identity. Only then should the conversation turn to institutional brand identity.

Because program heads' greatest fear is that central administration will eliminate their autonomy, institutions need to communicate the opposite. Most program heads were hired to make their programs succeed—and they were assured that they would receive all the support they needed. When advancement and marketing people appear to be controlling their communication, they naturally protest or at least become sullen and uncooperative. Marketing people who behave like logo police are dead in the water. They need to establish a different climate.

A PROCESS FOR CLARIFYING BRAND

Designing the right process for clarifying brand is an institution-specific task that relates to management culture and how employees expect to participate. Some participation is essential everywhere, but the level of participation can vary widely.

One approach is to have many different groups perform the same exercise, then compile the results and send the findings back to the groups for comment. Form focus groups composed of students, faculty, staff, administrators, alumni, donors, and trustees. Include a community group or two, either representatives of larger bodies or invited leaders. In some cases, one group representing designated priority groups works fine. It depends on organizational culture and expectations. What matters is that when the process is complete, all accept the results.

A FORMAT FOR DECISION-MAKING

Have each group perform four tasks:
1. List and prioritize five or six themes that best encapsulate the institution's strengths/distinctions.

2. List and prioritize the factors that establish the validity of these themes.
3. List the campus statues, landmarks, symbols, colors, design, architectural features, and any other elements that best express these themes.
4. Write one sentence that states the themes and establishes competitive advantage.

Introduce each group to branding and remind them of the results of the audit. Put each small group at a round table and give them the questions one at a time. Do not allow them to move on to the next question until they have finished the previous one. Give them a 30- to 45-minute time limit. If you schedule report-back sessions following each question, this exercise can take the better part of a day. But you can shorten the process by scheduling a single report-back session at the end.

After each group has recorded its results, facilitators collect them and create a composite "message-on-a-page." A week later, send this document to the participants, requesting their comments. Make edits based on the comments, and produce a final message-on-a-page. If other groups have performed the same exercise, compare their submissions and edit them into one final document. Present the final document to the president's cabinet for review and approval.

> Message-on-a-page is a concise statement of your competitive advantage, the themes that give it substance, the facts that prove it, and the campus and design elements that have or will come to symbolize it. It is used to get everyone telling the same story, which maximizes the power of word-of-mouth.

This message-on-a-page is a critical tool for integrated marketing programs. All professionals should have one on their desks to guide their daily work. Its points may be used verbatim in speeches and on fact sheets. Or they can serve as reminders that everything everyone in the institution communicates must reinforce these key reputation-defining themes. This applies to stories in our own publications as well as to stories pitched to the media. This is the way brands get built.

While the process varies among institutions, participants in those I have facilitated usually say they enjoy them much more than they expected. One president had his entire group of vice presidents, deans, other key administrators, and some faculty leaders spend the better part of a day in this kind of discussion. He introduced me in the morning session, saying, "It has been a long time since I have asked this group of high-powered people to take so much time off the job—so this better be good." I never have worked under so much pressure, but the day went very well. Even though executives generally avoid small-group discussions, they enjoyed these because they addressed a subject they dearly loved: What makes their institution special.

Do not tell executives in advance that you are going to put them into small discussion groups. Many will find legitimate reasons to bow out, even when the president has asked them to attend. But when the president invites them to a retreat aimed at clarifying the identity of the institution, and when they assume it will cost money that otherwise might come to them, they do attend. Once they arrive, they miraculously do not argue for their special interests. In fact, they usually do discuss the future of the entire university and gain a better understanding of what it will take to secure it.

In the case above, the chair of the board's marketing committee delivered opening remarks that reinforced the importance of the task at hand. He also stayed the entire day and participated in the discussions. That made the experience even more effective and paved the way for an entire integrated marketing program.

BREAKING DOWN SILOS

Historically, in most institutions and especially in large public ones, each school and college has operated as a "tub on its own bottom." Many deans act as if they were presidents, taking a dominant role in running their programs. Many deans believe that their schools alone can raise the prestige and visibility of the entire institution. One dean offered to cooperate with the centralized marketing initiative only if he was promised that it would not cost his school any old or new resources.

It can be very difficult to change this way of thinking, but over time and with persistence it can be done. And to remain competitive in the future, it will have to be done. There are few if any cases in which one college has established the reputation of an entire university. Usually, the institution's reputation represents the ceiling for all its programs. Only when the ceiling rises can the entities within take off. And that means everyone has to work together to strengthen the overall brand.

CHAPTER 6

GETTING INTEGRATED

After working in higher education for many years, it gradually occurred to me that universities are like small cities. We have our own police, utilities, garbage collection, and an array of people who think differently about a lot of things.

Academic institutions are not like other organizations. Members of the faculty think and behave independently, as do students. Members of the staff rarely consider themselves employees in the same sense as personnel in businesses. Rather, most staff members are supporters of a cause who relish the opportunity to join a community of independent thinkers. University executives control only the people who report to them, and these people too expect collegial treatment.

Chief executive officers in academic institutions rely more on persuasion than on force. When they are forced out of office, it is rarely because the board of trustees has become disenchanted with them. More often, the faculty has lost faith in them and has taken a public vote of "no confidence," eventually terminating the CEO's ability to govern.

THE NEED FOR INTEGRATED PROCESSES

Even given the political climate, academic institutions are organized around reporting channels and departments. Absent strong centralized control, the various units often become boxes that isolate people from each other. It is usually difficult to escape from those boxes and cultivate the working relationships essential for addressing organization-wide issues.

When external factors prompt fundamental changes in the institution, the institution must get the right people to work interactively on the most pressing challenges. Getting people to focus on agreed-on priorities and work cooperatively on the right projects requires integrated processes outside normal reporting channels. While this is true for many kinds of organizations, it is especially true for city-like academies.

Within this city-like environment, internal groups often compete for resources and prestige more intensely than in other environments. Because schools, colleges, and academic programs can become intensely competitive—especially at budget time—institutions must clarify exactly where they must compete for resources and where teamwork is expected. To address the problems facing the entire enterprise, institutions must establish a process to form working relationships purely for the greater good.

AN INTEGRATED TASK FORCE

Under my broad definition of marketing, the initial integrating entity is a marketing task force. Because this group must regard advancing the entire institution as its charge, it must be an integrated university-wide task force that includes all areas of advancement and everyone involved in communication and marketing.

The task force should first ask, "What major issue should we address to move the institution ahead?" In some cases, it will be enrollment; in others, an urgent need to raise more money; and in still others, the desire to establish brand identity, build reputation, and raise visibility.

In terms of organizational dynamics, when launching a new task force it is usually effective to have some kind of urgent "peg." The peg can be a response to an enrollment decline, the start of a fund-raising campaign, or complaints about lack of visibility. It can also be a new CEO's initiative to launch a new day with a brand new administration, or the current administrative team's announcement of an organizational renewal project.

To be effective, these task forces require the support of the entire executive team. The people invited to serve will do so energetically only if they feel their bosses expect it of them. The CEO should announce the project and invite its members. The CEO should also appoint a chair who can champion the process to the academic community, kick off the first meeting, periodically attend other meetings, and receive regular reports from the group.

Chairs need to understand all advancement disciplines, explain marketing in terms academics will understand, and earn the respect of other professionals and the faculty. Chairs must hold their own with the executive team, although they do not necessarily have to be formal members of it. Chairs must work with deans and students.

Finding the right chair is difficult, but the difficulty emphasizes the need to develop more sophisticated leadership in our fields. As mentioned earlier, the continuing education division is a good place to look, and sometimes a faculty member is a good choice. But the right chair usually comes directly from marketing and communication, persuasive evidence that the field has in a relatively short time evolved from providing services to producing leaders.

Task forces initially will consist of representatives from every on-campus unit that has a stake in marketing. Along with the marketing department itself, that includes communication, fund raising, alumni relations, admissions, continuing education, student affairs, the business office, athletics, the academic administration, faculty, students, bookstore, and the even campus police. One university has the campus police report to marketing because it views "community policing" and greeting visitors as important roles for police.

The criteria for task-force member selection should be overall talent as well as understanding of and interest in marketing and all other advancement areas. The task force will need energy and commitment to make things happen and to orchestrate special initiatives. This is not just a way to get department heads together; it should harness talent wherever it is found. Consider any staff members who volunteer to serve, especially if they exhibit a knack for marketing and a passion for the business.

I have found that personnel in many areas of universities are interested in and skilled at communication and marketing. They are not always professionally trained, but with professional leadership they quickly pick it up, love to participate, and help get the job done. So often advancement and marketing people feel they lack sufficient staff to do all the work. This task-force approach proves that the resources are there if you look for them, educate them, and free them to perform.

After brainstorming and identifying major issues, the task force will focus on priorities and consider what needs to be done. The primary need is almost always to clarify the institution's unique strengths, its competitive advantage. (See the audit exercise described in Chapter 4.) Once the message is clarified, the next most pressing need is to get everyone to understand, embrace, and communicate it. (Chapter 7 outlines initiatives for doing this.) Beyond these two concerns lies a number of priority targets—enrollment, campaign preparation, increased visibility, higher attendance at events, increased alumni involvement, higher student retention, better integration of technology, and just about anything. Because the list can get quite long, the task force must identify the two, three, or four most crucial ones.

FORMING ACTION TEAMS

Task forces often form action teams to study, launch, and evaluate specific initiatives. Action teams have helped move organizations ahead and will help even more in the future. They focus on priority initiatives and harness the best talent in the organization to do the job. I believe action teams will be formed by all kinds of organizations, from governments to nongovernmental organizations (NGOs), to penetrate the media clutter and spread the word that the institution is stepping out and making a difference. Organizations benefit when external people say, "Look what they are doing; they are really taking off."

Action teams should recruit someone who knows what research has been performed in its particular area of concern. They should have a strategic planner, and they should have a member who has hands-on experience with the issue or eventual audience.

Because the creators of the materials need to participate in the development of ideas, action teams should at the outset involve both a writer and a designer. Their experience and insights will be invaluable all through the process. The copy and design always will be more effective when writers and designers are on the scene from the start. When writers are called in later, their copy may seem off the mark. Designers often are brought in even later, often too late in the process to produce concept ideas. But when a talented designer has been present throughout the developmental process and has watched the entire process unfold, the first design is often the best.

Action teams should concentrate on developing special initiatives. For example, if the goal is to increase enrollment, they can focus on identifying and locating the problem, determining which tactics are likely to make the biggest difference, and then constructing an integrated communication assault. Teams should review relevant research and, on occasion, request new research. Teams also should review possible tactics, selecting those that produce synergistic impact and creating a mechanism for evaluating results.

A combination of direct mail—snailmail and e-mail—and advertising could converge simultaneously on a target. Or a combination of radio ads, billboards, and shopping-mall posters could target the same audience. The purpose: to create enough convergence and intensity to penetrate the information and media clutter.

Action teams also can find ways to use internal communication and marketing to get people on the same page, prepare various units for a campaign, broaden and increase alumni participation, and increase visibility.

INCREASING VISIBILITY

How many advancement professionals have been told that their institution is the "best-kept secret" in town? Even administrators at well-known institutions hear this from alumni leaders and donors.

Perversely, the closer someone is to an institution the more they see its competitor's communication. They resent the other institution's visibility and want to see their own institution's name hanging from the sky everywhere they go. But in today's information-cluttered world, more communication adds to the clutter, and few institutions, if any, can afford enough targeted and saturated media to establish a national and international presence.

The solution to the visibility problem, therefore, is a strategic one. If the people who will be responsible for sustaining the institution believe it is visible, then for all practical purposes it is visible. Institutions must identify and locate these people—prospective students, parents, alumni leaders, donors, legislators, media gatekeepers, high school counselors, and others—and make sure communication from various sources converges on them with enough intensity to make the institution a household name. A talented visibility action team can achieve this objective.

EVALUATING RESULTS

Unless you stick to the numbers, evaluating results is particularly difficult in the advancement professions. Certainly, if enrollment increases or you achieve your fund-raising goal, you have succeeded. But even then people may say, "Could we have done that without all that advertising?" Or, "What if we had not done all those college fairs?" Some will always say the word got out because we are good, and, "If you build it they will come."

Wrong. They don't just come. Maybe it used to be true, but in higher education today it does not work that way. To attract students, institutions must offer the right product and connect with the right people.

That's what marketing and communication will be all about. And it will take a convergence of media to attract attention and elicit responses.

The best evaluations use as much interactive media as possible, in which case the communication process itself comprises much of the evaluation. Feedback is instant, and you can adjust the message as you go. But as people get more involved with task forces and action teams, the more accurately they assess—along with the professionals—what is and is not working.

It is interesting to observe different institutions. Where top executives or trustees force marketing, communication, and advancement people to prove they are effective, strategic marketing rarely moves forward. That is because leaders know that marketing works only when they participate in or empathize with the process. Numbers arguments never satisfy. If the objective is to find ways to cut the budget, leadership will assume that programs are responsible for their own success and that marketing may not have been necessary.

But when top people are deeply involved and the process yields better results, enhanced marketing usually gets the credit. People close to the process are in touch with its dynamics. Collective determination usually exists to keep the initiatives coming and the institution moving. Just as retaining repeat customers costs less than obtaining new ones, retaining the right kind of visibility costs less than starting from scratch.

EDITORIAL PRIORITIES COMMITTEES

Improving the coordination of the daily flow of information is part of this process. Because an academic institution is like a city, it generates all kinds of information every day. Distributing it certainly contributes to the clutter.

The process of establishing identity and brand by choosing the themes that will produce clarity also provides thematic guidelines for editing and coordinating the daily information flow. Some news goes out just because it is daily news, that is, accomplishments, events, etc. But the stories you select to pitch to the media, feature in the magazine, lead e-mail newsletters, or headline the Web site should reinforce the themes that define the brand.

I call these stories "reputation defining" because they are told repeatedly and verify the institution's claims of distinction. In the past, many professionals thought that once they told a story they could never tell it again, or at least not tell it for a while. Today, to break through the clutter, the big stories must be told over and over again in every medium, repeated in speeches, and featured in magazines, videos, and everywhere feasible.

Editorial priorities committees consist of the staff who write official materials. They meet—sometimes monthly, sometimes weekly—to select reputation-defining stories, make sure they all have the same stories, and coordinate the ways those stories are told. They use the message-on-a-page described in Chapter 5 as their guiding document.

THE POWER OF INTEGRATION

The power of integration derives from the dynamics of the creative group process. Integration mobilizes talent and focuses it on priority objectives. It can put an institution on the map, at least in the minds of stakeholders, and it can make it more competitive in every way.

Integration harnesses talent and combines resources to improve efficiency. When athletics are integrated with the institution, the institution treats athletics as a part of the total campus experience, and the athletics department remembers its responsibility to advance the entire institution. Integration unites disparate units and divisions into a coordinated whole, helping external people appreciate the strengths and support the contributions of the entire organization.

FINDING PARTNERS EVERYWHERE

I mentioned earlier the power of partnerships. Partnerships with media outlets, performing arts organizations, and service agencies provide instant, cost-effective visibility and stature. Often these partners can be productive members of integrated task forces and special-cases action teams. Their perspective and expertise quickly become an inexpensive way of accessing otherwise costly outside talent.

Furthermore, this process makes partners of everyone involved. Every member of any of these groups feels an enduring sense of partnership. Work becomes more productive, the institution becomes more successful, and everyone has more fun. In the days and years ahead, academic advancement activities will have to become more strategic and more targeted.

CHAPTER 7

BUILDING INTERNAL CULTURE

To meet the challenges of the future, the entire internal community must understand the external forces that are producing dramatic changes in the educational marketplace. Moreover, the internal community must reach a consensus about what the institution should do. Educational institutions will not be insulated from outside bombardments or competitive economic forces. Academic freedom will remain a fundamental concept for scholars, but finding enough of the right students and enough resources to support their work will be a big challenge—a responsibility that must be shared by everyone, not just the professionals who will lead the effort.

This means the academy will require a lot more communication and a lot more interaction. It means installing processes that unify people and messages, and it means involving units ranging from marketing and communication to human resources and student affairs. Although it will be more important than ever, casual interaction will no longer be enough. Units will have to orchestrate communication and marketing with clear competitive objectives.

INTEGRATED MARKETING LEADS INTERNALLY

Once an institution launches an integrated marketing program, it quickly becomes apparent that internal communication will require additional staff time and resources. While institutions have long recognized the importance of internal communication, it never seems to be allocated enough staff time and effort—at least in most institutions. The analytical processes of integrated marketing not only disclose the need for a more sophisticated and comprehensive program, they also indicate that it is absolutely imperative.

Indeed, external communication demands are acute, and meeting them can take all the effort a communications office can muster. After external materials are produced and releases distributed, there just is not any more time. But this is the case only when organizations view external communication as the top and only priority and do not understand that strong internal communication can facilitate strong external communication. In fact, internal communication is the most powerful kind of word-of-mouth external communication, which can be a positive or negative depending on what internal people are saying. Getting internal communication right is prerequisite for everything else. It is *the* best mechanism for getting everyone on the same page and motivating them to tell the right story.

COMMUNICATIONS VS. MARKETING

When marketing enters the picture, internal communication objectives expand. Because early discussions always indicate that marketing cannot succeed without effective internal communication, internal marketing activities are quickly initiated.

As explained previously, internal communication seeks to improve the flow of information about news and events and build a sense of community with human-interest stories. As differentiated from communication, effective internal marketing gets everyone to agree on brand identity and competitive advantage, and it motivates internal and external word-of-mouth support. They are separate but highly coordinated activities.

Good internal communication means having the right media in place to keep the community informed and, to some extent, bonded. Internal newsletters and bulletins, posters and kiosks, tabloid publications, and electronic media inform the community about events, activities, and human interests. While much of the media concisely conveys information, some items pique interest in the professional and personal lives of people in the institutional family.

Internal communication is used to explain organizational policies and workplace benefits. And today, staff use internal communication media such as hotlines and Web sites to discuss critical issues and offer suggestions for organizational improvement. Supervisors and managers also use regular and periodic news bulletins to disseminate vital information to employees.

THE POWER OF 'ON A MISSION'

In addition to producing the customary internal communication media, internal marketing adds a number of new initiatives to the mix. This begins with clearly defining the institutional identity message. The foundation of that message is the mission statement.

The ultimate purpose of the mission statement is to make everyone understand what makes the institution unique or at least distinctive. As explained previously, that distinction is its claimed competitive advantage. The origin of this claim should appear in the founding mission, and the mission should be made forward-looking with an accompanying vision statement. For internal purposes, a clear mission statement that flows into a more comprehensive message-on-a-page will provide the substance of an internal marketing initiative that will unite the community and build a corporate culture with clear values and traditions.

INTERNAL MARKETING INSPIRES NEW ACTIVITIES

Internal marketing finds new ways to communicate the mission statement and message-on-a-page on campus. It does this as interactively as possible, placing strong emphasis on participation and commitment to a cause.

Internal special events are critical. Internal events inspire renewed commitment to the institution's mission. One institution holds a kickoff luncheon each fall for all faculty and staff, reinforcing the mission with mugs, bookmarks, T-shirts, and other promotional items. Onsite banners remind faculty and staff of the mission. Staff nominated for special recognition based on their service to the mission throughout the year are honored at this luncheon. Their contributions also are acclaimed in periodicals, and they receive commendations handdelivered by the president.

Getting the mission into the campus environment year-round is a major task of internal marketing. The kickoff-luncheon banners can be used at other events, displayed in building lobbies, and situated in other areas of the campus to spread awareness of the mission. Other themes from the message-on-a-page can be placed on posters and message boards in public areas.

START AT ORIENTATION

The best time to begin the internal marketing and communication process is when new staff join the institution. Everyone wants to believe they have made a great career choice. Excited about beginning a new chapter of their lives, they are most receptive to anything that will help them enjoy their tenure and succeed. More than any other time, this is when they will respond to messages that explain why the institution is special.

Unfortunately, few employee or faculty orientation programs address institutional marketing. They discuss procedures, major policies, and benefits. They explain the medical plan, retirement benefits, and alternative insurance plans. One institution points out building entrances and where restrooms are located. And while some orientation programs provide lists of the publications each employee will receive, few discuss the marketing plan, factors that make the place special, and what the institution is doing to remain competitive.

Orientation programs can easily describe the mission, vision, and values summarized in the message-on-a-page. They can also explain how the message-on-a-page influences all official materials and emphasize that every staff member is responsible for telling the story. Orientation programs can cite examples of employees who incorporate the major message points into conversations with friends, explain institutional actions in staff meetings, and deliver presentations at professional associations, local clubs, and churches.

Giving new employees materials, even gifts, as reminders also is effective. For example, the marketing and communication department could give them a briefcase inscribed with its elegant logo, a coffee cup bearing the mission statement, or framed versions of the mission, vision, and values statements. Inside the briefcase, place a copy of the message-on-a-page and a guide to the procedures for requesting assistance on marketing or communication matters—including policies about contacting or responding to the media.

While there are many ways to do this in a focused way in a brief period of time, do not forget that new-employee orientation is the ideal place to mobilize the troops that will strive for competitive success in the years ahead. Getting to them before they develop biases about the organization, fall under the influence of the committed complainers, or allow their own cynical tendencies to take over is a critical step toward creating an overall positive outlook and cultivating willingness to help.

CUSTOMER-SERVICE EDUCATION

In today's service-oriented world, institutions will have to satisfy the student and parent expectations that have been shaped by modern living, especially in the areas of housing, food services, and all business transactions. In the area of academics, expectations are less clear. They definitely include, however, personal access to faculty, sensitivity to individual needs, and help to solve all kinds of problems. This is a service economy, and "customers" expect good service. And while everyone avoids calling a student a "customer," in all of these ways they and their parents expect to be treated as such. And so, there is no doubt that delivering great service establishes an important competitive advantage in this increasingly competitive marketplace.

The quality of facilities and the products that back up the services will become much more important. Our food quality, pricing, and delivery will be compared to off-campus venues. Our recreation and sports-center equipment will be compared to outside fitness clubs and gyms, as will the level of service at these facilities. Our career-service centers will need not only the latest information and software but also people who treat students like professional clients. The same goes for our medical centers, counseling centers, and other units that provide student services.

Staff in the business, financial aid, and registrar's offices will be expected to deliver the same kind of service consumers expect from banks, credit offices, and insurance firms. We may complain about poorly staffed banks and financially troubled airlines, but we still expect pleasant, positive, and helpful treatment. This service attitude will establish a critical competitive advantage with our "new customers" that translates into improved student retention. Retention is a complicated issue, and some students leave for specific, legitimate reasons. But an overall sense of belonging is often a factor, and quality of service plays a large role in creating that feeling.

DEVELOPING A SERVICE CULTURE

The kind of customer-service training that exists in the commercial world may not work in the academy. Some people choose to work in academic institutions because they do not want to be told how to do everything. Others regard students as older children and consider it demeaning to treat them like customers. And still others think of themselves "idea people" who should be making the decisions and do not need a how-to-do-it training program.

I have been a part of a failed experiment to adapt a commercial customer-service program to a university setting. The program was adapted for our use but not adapted well enough. Administrative office personnel resented receiving elementary instructions about answering phones and greeting walk-ins. Our employees felt we were talking down to them, thought the examples simplistic, and generally found the material silly and unrelated to their interaction with students and parents.

A better approach is to hold employee group meetings where problems are identified, solutions reached through brainstorming, and courses of action collectively outlined. During the conversations, meeting facilitators remark on the competitive marketplace and how the issues at hand are critical to the institution's survival, let alone its success. The message-on-a-page can be distributed as a helpful informational resource, and later on someone from marketing could brief employees on how tough it is out there today and how the institution is handling the situation.

"Appreciative inquiry" is a new approach to solving problems that does not involve addressing problems directly. Rather, people are asked to identify what they have done that has worked effectively in their areas, activities and initiatives that pleased them and the people they serve. Then they determine ways to do more of the same, trusting that the underlying problems will diminish or disappear as a result. Appreciative inquiry establishes a consistently positive climate in the office, as opposed to the negative atmosphere that results from adopting a negative attitude about problems.

"Customer service" might better be called "student service" or something else. In the academy, people over-debate the definition of terms and always find academic objections to their usage. But because of the widespread, unyielding aversion to treating students as "customers," we might as well call it just plain "service" and define it as "helping people get what they need in a spirit of good cheer." Developing campus-wide sensitivity to whatever we call it will be critical to remaining viable as an organization.

MAKE FRIENDS IN HR

You will notice that the last several topics, from new-employee orientation to customer-service education, all assume a traditional role for the human resources area. The next topic of management communication has implications for HR as well.

In the past, few marketing and communication departments have maintained daily working relationships with HR. Integrated marketing and communication objectives change all that dramatically. Now, integrated marketing and communication has to work with HR to plan new-employee orientation, customer-service discussion meetings, and possibly management-training sessions on the communication responsibilities of supervisors and managers, and ways to deliver sensitive information face-to-face.

THE ROLE OF MANAGEMENT COMMUNICATION

Most people want to receive work-related information directly from the person to whom they report. If they get it from another source, they often deny knowing it. They seldom try to verify what they hear; rather, they just blame management for not telling them. "They didn't tell me" becomes a form of personal protection—that is, "What I didn't know, they can't blame me for." This psychological mechanism masks fear of inefficiency.

To make matters worse, memos from top management on important or sensitive subjects, no matter how carefully worded, usually generate rampant misunderstanding. This is because the more carefully crafted a document, the more suspicion it generates. Worse, most people will not read it carefully, but rather scan it quickly to confirm whatever biases they already hold. Rumors spread, even though much care was taken to make the memo clear.

Do not assume the office of communication can spread the word about work-related policies and benefits. The office of communication can communicate information about events, individual achievements, and daily activities. It can tell human-interest stories and even fulfill internal marketing objectives. And while it can report on events and issues related to policy- or work-related matters, communicating the substance of the action is the responsibility of management.

TACTICS FOR MANAGEMENT COMMUNICATION

First, make sure managers and supervisors know they are expected to communicate all work-related and sensitive information face-to-face with their employees. Then provide the education and training they will need to do it effectively—something most university HR offices have never done. Most academic institutions teach about education but provide little management education to their own administrators, faculty, and employees. Here communication professionals can help. Communication professionals can do some of that training through HR or help HR find faculty members or outside consultants who can do it. A partnership between HR and integrated marketing and communication can make sure the right issues are addressed and the right skills taught.

Other processes also can facilitate effective communication. The president can establish an administrative council made up of the vice presidents and most of the people who report to them. This group can meet monthly or quarterly to review critical issues that need to be communicated and discuss ways to communicate them effectively. In so doing, the president effectively communicates his or her personal theme and personally oversees the group primarily responsible for delivering the message. Regular e-mail reports to the council and "blasts" to all staff and faculty facilitate effective communication. But it must take place face-to-face, and it will never happen if managers and supervisors fail to do their part.

Executive briefings, town hall meetings, and casual office visits help establish a climate of open communication. While that kind of climate fosters success and molds a productive corporate culture, nothing replaces the manager or supervisor. Nothing.

COMMUNICATING WITH STUDENTS

Most institutions find it difficult, if not impossible, to communicate effectively with students. Student newspapers certainly don't do it. They report the news and, like metropolitan dailies, do not feel obliged to keep students informed about the institution. Even if they did, most students would not see the information when the institution needed them to see it.

In-house newsletters rarely reach most students. The distribution process is problematic, and if they get them they seldom read them. If you send information to their personal mailboxes, many pieces wind up on the floor of the campus post office. E-surveys, e-mail messages, electronic news boards, kiosks, and posters all have limited success in disseminating messages. You must continue to make the effort, but effective communication with the student body seldom exists.

Another approach is word-of-mouth. When messages are clearly defined, word-of-mouth can reach campus leaders. For example, internal marketing and communication operations can have student leaders make reports directly to student groups, with modest payments or food given to participants. Such student "ambassadors" can pave the way for staff members to talk to student groups or deliver reports at their meetings.

Liaisons with student government can work the same way. Some professionals are logging into student Internet chat rooms. While some may consider this manipulative, it is an intriguing way to reach students that might get them to respond. This technique will no doubt become a greater part of institutional marketing practices as well.

APPARENT TRANSPARENCY

Internal communication creates an atmosphere of transparency—to make it seem that the information anyone needs is readily available and that relevant parties participate in decision making. Systems that work properly have transparency. Everyone gets what they need from supervisors and can participate in making the decisions that affect them.

But in effectively managed organizations, total transparency is not always possible. Some information—information on students and personnel, for example—might be considered privileged. Other information may be readily available to those it concerns but not to others. For example, the early drafts of a special planning committee report might describe developments that may never occur or emphasize issues that turn out to be immaterial. This is of special concern in areas where ambitious reporters in search of scoops can jump the gun and misinform the public. When that happens, no interests are served and widespread misunderstandings are almost impossible to correct.

In other words, honest, factual, clear communication requires management. But managing does not mean manipulating the outcome. Rather, it means ensuring that appropriate parties have access to information, and that the most credible sources communicate clearly and accurately.

ORCHESTRATING INTERNAL COMMUNICATION

Internal communication reports what goes on inside the institution, gets everyone on the same page with respect to identity and competitive advantage, and then motivates them to go out and tell the story. Equally important, internal communication shapes and reaffirms the institution's corporate culture, a service-oriented culture with clearly defined and well-established communication processes.

When it all comes together, thousands of highly motivated communicators tell the right story to the right people at the right time. That creates a positive image ("Did you hear about the great things happening out there?") and brand—the most effective marketing dynamic an organization can have. In the future, academic institutions will strive to become both self-perpetuating and accessible: self-perpetuating because staff and alumni will encourage families and friends to attend and support the institution, and accessible because anyone who qualifies will be able to attend. The more attractive an institution is to those nearby, the more attractive it will be to others. But it will be attractive only when the communication process is well orchestrated and well led. "Build it and they will come" no longer works in a competitive world.

CHAPTER 8

ONGOING RESEARCH

Few people have a natural understanding of marketing. Many in higher education still honestly believe that "if you build it they will come." Even more think marketing is merely a matter of telling people what you have. Few understand that it is an organizational dynamic, and that it must be orchestrated.

The process begins with viewing the world as separate audiences, or market segments, and understanding where the members of each segment stand in relation to your institution. Have they heard of it at all (awareness)? If so, do they have a positive or negative impression (attitude)? If positive, do they understand what differentiates you from other institutions (knowledge)? If they understand, do they see how your institution will meet their needs (connection factors)? What will it take to meet their needs, as you plan to show them how you will meet needs they do not know they had? Answering these and other questions requires marketing research.

The situation gets complicated because markets are constantly changing, especially the younger markets. Basic characteristics change every few years, and as soon as we understand one change, a new change materializes. Certainly, no one can consistently trust his or her own judgment about what will and will not work. The professional approach to advancement work has been to build ongoing marketing research programs; in the future, such programs will need to be built solidly into marketing and communication operations.

ONGOING RESEARCH TACTICS

Communication initiatives and channels should offer audiences opportunities to respond. When you communicate with a market segment, whenever possible request feedback and be prepared to collect and categorize the information you receive. If you ask questions in the communications you disseminate, the events you evaluate, the calls you make, and the e-mails you send, you can collect information in a systematic way. You begin to understand your markets by living and working in the communication process.

What most people do not understand about marketing people is that they really do "live in the communication process" and thus develop a feel for what will or will not succeed. They see and feel what is happening in the marketplace every day. When one is challenged to "prove that the advertisement was worth the money," it is almost always impossible to do it in quantitative terms. But professionals who "live in the communication process" sense over time whether media are producing the synergy that maximizes results. It comes from a combination of judgment and information derived from ongoing, interactive communication and research. Involving more people in integrated marketing processes lets the entire advancement staff understand better what is working.

OTHER BASIC TECHNIQUES

Traditional research techniques that will remain useful include written surveys, telephone surveys, e-surveys, and focus groups.

Written surveys. Written surveys are rarely used because they seldom generate valid response rates. Exceptions include written surveys used for personal interviews, operations-effectiveness audits, and studies of homogenous groups that will reliably respond. Written surveys accommodate lengthy, thoughtful responses. But use them only when you have a captive audience in a setting and a time-frame conducive to thorough responses.

Telephone surveys. Professional research firms favor telephone interviews conducted by trained callers because they can keep calling until they have enough responses to ensure statistical reliability. The size of the calling sample and the length of the questionnaire determine the cost of telephone-based research. Fewer, more focused questions mean less expensive projects.

When you stick with one target market and a small set of questions, it is possible to do telephone surveys on a modest budget. A greater number of smaller focused studies is preferable to large comprehensive ones. Large studies are very costly, and they often confirm only what you already know, which creates confusion when it comes to making decisions. Resist the wouldn't-it-be-nice-to-know mind-set that can make survey projects large and cumbersome. Smaller, focused surveys that ask only a few actionable questions are less expensive. And repeating them periodically helps you establish trend lines, which are instrumental to good decision-making over time.

Survey clearinghouse. In most institutions, academic and support departments all over campus conduct their own surveys. Frankly, many are poorly done and pretty much worthless. Others have limited validity. But by performing an inventory of who is doing what, you can determine what is collectively known about the institution and ways to use better the combined resources spent on institutional research. Institutions almost always have more information already available than anyone realizes.

Data mining. A lot of data is available everywhere, both inside and outside the institution. Mining, or systematically analyzing that data, is very useful and very economical. The Internet can access information on generational characteristics, economic and social trends, competing institutions, and more. An able person who pulls together internal data and statistics collected by people throughout the organization can match social needs with institutional strengths, write people-profiles that guide admissions on how and where to find similar people, and much more. It is wise to have someone in your organization regularly compile databases.

DEVELOPING TREND LINES

Daily changing admissions indicators make it difficult to predict future enrollment accurately. Based on numbers at a certain point in the process, it used to be possible to predict the number of students who showed up and which ones they would be. It also used to be possible to know exactly what submitting an application meant to students. Now every prospect applies to so many places that it is impossible to know whether applications signify genuine interest. To predict behavior, it is necessary to track behavioral trends.

Marketing research directors on the staff of marketing and communication operations will formulate a schedule of research projects and collect information on student recruiting, reputation building, alumni, donors, and community leaders on a regular and systematic basis. Some studies will assess the internal climate and address the complex matter of student retention. Some studies will be repeated annually, others every two or three years. Research directors will conduct some studies themselves, while others will be outsourced to consultants. But someone will have to manage the collection of information on the changing marketplace on a daily basis.

AWARENESS, ATTITUDE, AND KNOWLEDGE

While you will want to get all kinds of information about your target markets, you basically need to find out whether people know you exist, like what they see, and are aware of your strengths. Of the three, the last is the least important, but some aspects are of concern.

Ultimately, you will be surprised and disappointed by what even your closest and most active volunteers don't know about your institution. You will be constantly amazed that so many can find out so much and know so little. But they should at least know the basic characteristics that comprise your competitive advantage. What differentiates you and makes you better is the brand identity that will establish pride and eventually cultivate loyalty. And loyalty will be more important than ever in the new, redefined world of higher education, where there will be more competition for your donor's time and money, your alumni children's applications, and prestige in the eye of your stakeholders.

It all begins with awareness. If key people in target markets have never heard of you, making them aware of you comes first. Many institutions use intercollegiate athletics to achieve the widespread name recognition that paves the way for marketing. Of course, there are other ways to create awareness, but, depending on your institution's overall market size, athletics may be less expensive than purchasing visibility in other ways. Many institutions now feel the cost versus benefit of media saturation is getting too high, and eventually something will have to change.

Once you achieve awareness and verify it with research, the next step is to establish a positive image. As stated elsewhere, a positive image is not a pretty photo; it is the perception that "exciting things are going on out there." Conversely, a negative image is, "They have problems out there." After institutions confirm that they have a positive image in each market, they then must communicate the themes that comprise their competitive advantage.

Monitoring this requires an ongoing research program; telephone surveys are usually the best tool. Have research professionals design the questionnaires, have trained callers make the calls, and use experienced analysts to crunch the data. But you can do all this and still get bad information. Focus groups can help design the questionnaire before the study and add details afterward. One-on-one interviews can also be effective.

Surveys aimed at prospective students, parents, alumni, donors, legislators, and community leaders are becoming critically important. Research thus becomes a basic tool of professionals in this intense and increasingly international field.

LOST BUSINESS
Some of the most valuable data come from students who were admitted to your institution but chose to attend elsewhere—if you can find

them. While they may be attending any of hundreds of other schools, you can reach them at their home address at holiday time. Of course, interviewing their parents can be enlightening as well.

Because respondents often give the easy answer rather than the honest one, engage professionals to write questions that get past those psychological barriers. Knowing why students you accepted went elsewhere is critically important for improving the perception of your overall value and providing services related to living on or near campus. Do not accept "you were just too expensive" as the definitive answer. Sometimes it is, but often it is an easy way of saying they did not believe your institution was worth the trouble of figuring out how to pay for it.

PRICING ELASTICITY

Price is the most complicated marketing factor in our industry today. People are confused about what an education should cost and how much they should have to pay. Studies by professional associations and independent opinion research organizations consistently find that the public thinks that institutions are ineffectively managed and that they can cut costs without sacrificing quality. People generally believe tuition pays the entire cost of an education; they do not understand how endowments and donors subsidize the enterprise. They think large endowments mean institutions are wealthy. And when any institution—a lower-priced public university or an expensive private school—raises its price, many feel they no longer can afford it.

Price, in fact, does have some relation to the revenue needed to run the institution. But price also is determined partly by the way the price influences perceptions of quality. Many schools try hard to maintain a "sticker price" that makes admission accessible to all students. Others use higher sticker prices to suggest a high level of quality and prestige, but they may cut the price by more than half to achieve desirable student-body diversity. Those institutions are convinced that they need the prestige of a higher price to compete in a high-quality market. Someone once said, "If you buy a Lexus priced too cheaply, you will worry that something's wrong with it. If you feel you got a good deal, however, you will be happy."

While all these marketing strategies can be effective, the public is still confused about price and value—and the situation gets more complicated every day. Some institutions, mostly pricey privates, will remain in a prestige market where they compete with similar schools. Others, mostly publics, will continue to compete in a market where they must maintain the perception of accessibility. But there are a great number of other schools, mostly private, that find themselves caught in the middle: They want to be perceived as a prestige choice in a market sector where most of their competitors are lower-priced, public institutions. These are the institutions that face the most complicated pricing dilemmas.

Research on pricing elasticity will tell you how much you can charge before consumer resistance seriously lowers enrollments. The results are usually stated as degrees of risk, from "fairly safe" to "high risk." Because it is not easy to obtain truthful information about what people are willing to pay, the structure of questions is critically important. Most people, regardless of their financial situation, come in with the attitude that your price already is too high.

Not too long ago, many groups were conducting pricing research. Several still do, but you need choose carefully and make sure you know in advance what the results will tell you. Because pricing conditions change every year, redo these studies regularly. The more studies you do, the better you will understand the trends in your particular market.

CUSTOMER SATISFACTION

Student retention is an issue that is likely to become even more prominent. Exit interviews yield little useful information, no doubt because students offer easy answers to justify decisions already made. Stated reasons commonly include family, girlfriends or boyfriends in other institutions, and cost, but the truth is usually much more complex.

The decision to leave an institution is made over time; it is a complex matter that often is related to feeling comfortable and fitting in. Sometimes individuals are uncomfortable with their living arrangements, or they may not have made a connection to an academic department. It can be a matter of not getting the right help at the right time. And, of course, there will always be a certain amount of justifiable attrition.

Customer-satisfaction research assesses feelings long before individuals decide to leave. It explores the environmental and service issues that define the total social and academic experience at the institution. It provides input on lifestyle matters such as food services, housing, and counseling. And it identifies problems related to student well-being in particular academic programs.

It is difficult to perform customer-satisfaction research in secret, and when people on campus find out about it, they will expect you to publish the results. Of course, asking level-of-satisfaction questions invites complaints, many of which are predictable. Campus food is a perennial target of complaints, as is parking. Many fear that this research merely will confirm what is already known and give fuel to the institution's critics.

Construct questionnaires that probe beyond typical complaints. You may conduct blind surveys that do not name your organization, or use targeted surveys that exclude typical complaint topics. Either way, discern and address the specific environmental elements that make students leave your institution before graduation. Exit interviews are not getting the information you need.

MEDIA PREFERENCE

Cutting through mass communication clutter requires focused and interactive messages. And it means knowing the media preferred by consumers in each market segment. Because research organizations perform annual studies on preferences and trends, standard demographic studies can tell you much of what you need to know.

But when you survey particular target markets, it is wise to throw in a question or two about media preferences. Yes, I already said not to clutter surveys with extra questions, but this is a rare exception. Do it with a single question that asks respondents to rank a list of media outlets in order of preference.

For example, to determine how many people in each market segment you can reach electronically, you must find out whether they have computers with online access and if they prefer to hear from you that way. While Internet use may be soaring, many people still prefer snailmail and hard copies. This seems to differ by generations, but it may also differ within generations. While prospective students may access your Web site early in the admission process to find out specific things about your institution, most still desire and expect traditional viewbooks and other print materials.

BEHAVIOR OBSERVATION

What people actually do is a better indication of what they will do in the future than what they say they will do. For example, television researchers do not ask what kind of programs people want to watch because respondents would tell them one thing and then watch something else. Instead, television researchers observe viewing behavior and then program more of the same.

Many institutions are concerned about gender balance. Schools with a growing number of females would like to attract more males. Clearly, the conventional wisdom that more females will attract more males does not work, nor does asking males what they want.

Consequently, some institutions systematically observe what males do on campus, especially on campuses that attract more of them. And while some of what they see cannot be used as an enticement, legitimate strategies can be abstracted. Apparently, college-age males want to feel independent and prefer to attend schools where groups of men live and socialize with other men. Campuses viewed as smaller and more protective are not as attractive to men, even if these campuses have more women. Systematic behavior observation no doubt will become a more important research tool.

MORE INTERNATIONAL

As our industry changes globally, the competitive landscape will begin to look very different. The international student market will involve much more than a handful of countries willing to send us students. Many countries are now building academic institutions to keep their talented young people home. More will recruit talented young Americans with the message, "We provide quality English-language programs that are Asia-aware—and that's where the exciting opportunities will be."

All this has serious research implications. What will your best markets be in a changing international environment? Do any new locations make sense for your institution? How can you get international students to respond to you? How can you keep the students you have when others ply them with enticements? Will that be enough? It may be, and it may be the wisest strategy for you. These are all research-related questions that will require information you can act on and understanding the information as it changes over time.

CHAPTER 9

FINDING ENOUGH OF
THE RIGHT STUDENTS

Government funding cutbacks affect everything. Fund raising becomes more important, but institutions also look at tuition pricing, which leads to marketing-related concerns about simultaneously maintaining access and increasing income. Thus begins evaluation of the entire admissions process:

- What are the characteristics of the best students for our institution?
- Where can we find more of them?
- How much can they afford to pay?
- How much financial aid will we need to remain accessible?

MORE TIES TO MARKETING, COMMUNICATION

When institutions launch integrated marketing programs, they usually first assemble a task force composed of every area of the institution engaged in some kind of marketing—from the bookstore to athletics to the schools and colleges to admissions and more. It quickly becomes clear that all marketing aims toward finding students, raising money, and building reputation. And of the three, finding students is the most basic; indeed, it is the foundation of the core business. Marketing and communication will naturally spend much of its time integrating operations with admissions.

Many institutions decide to restructure by placing admissions in the same administrative unit as marketing and communication. In some cases, this is a better administrative marriage than combining marketing and communication with fund raising and alumni relations. The key is to integrate all planning and implementation, whether or not departments are together in a formal administrative structure. The many factors that determine the best way to organize advancement areas are discussed in Chapter 14. But to become more competitive, many institutions will have to revise their organizational structures.

CONSUMERS' ROLE

The role of students and parents in higher education is changing all over the world. Students no longer are intimidated by universities. Only very high-performing students who seek admission to the most prestigious schools sit home hoping they will be accepted somewhere. Most average to very good students are in a good bargaining position these days, and they know it.

In many societies, and especially in the United States, cell phones permit parents and children to communicate more easily and collaborate more on everything, including the choice of college. Now in the United States, "helicopter parents" hover over their children, pose as their children to obtain information, sometimes write their children's essays, and certainly coach them through the admissions process.

Families obtain additional help from consultants, beginning with high school counselors who try to get the best students into the best schools and continuing with professional consultants who show families various ways to negotiate the best deal possible.

College choice often takes into consideration the institution as a travel destination. Family visits are no longer limited to parents' weekends. Because the family may visit campus five or six times a year, the entire city and its attractions become involved in the choice process. Admissions-marketing programs often include detailed information about hotels and city's cultural and tourist attractions.

BUILDING RELATIONSHIPS

The entire admissions process must aim at establishing a bond among parents and prospect and institution. By the time of matriculation, the family already should feel an emotional bond and a sense of commitment to the campus community: This is what branding is all about. Because prospects and their families no longer respond to arguments and persuasion, you have real competitive advantage only if, by the time they choose, they feel most comfortable on your campus. This holds true even for the best students. All of them want to establish a meaningful emotional connection with the institution they select.

SAFETY

Safety is a real issue in today's volatile and dangerous society. Concerned parents want to feel your campus is secure. While safety is a more significant factor with daughters than with sons, it is a universal concern. Thus it is critical to provide information on safety early on.

Many institutions have taken innovative steps to improve safety.

Along with upgrading fencing, lighting, and security patrols, they have initiated night escort services and installed electronic communication systems with easy outdoor access. This is marketing at its best: program development that establishes and communicates benefits consumers know they want and need.

CLEARER IDENTITY

Clarifying identity is a vitally important, but often unappreciated, aspect of higher-education marketing. In education, the institution's "brand" becomes the "product" students and parents buy.

Younger prospects who have decided on an academic field want to know that the institution offers a quality program in that area. But because many will change majors during the course of their educational careers, what they *really* want is an institution they can be proud to call their alma mater. While they may not fully appreciate this when they arrive on campus, they will carry the institution's identity with them for the rest of their lives.

All this provides additional substance for the marketing message: a clear compelling brand that will become a student's lifelong identity. This is why developing a powerful brand is a front-and-center concern of institutional marketers. Developing a powerful brand also establishes competitive advantage, which lets people take pride in the attributes that make their institution superior.

But the brand-building process also is changing, especially for younger generations. Evidence indicates that while young people are very brand-conscious and brand-driven, they themselves determine their own brand preferences and change them rapidly. A "school of choice" one moment may not be their choice the next. And because many of their decisions are based on word-of-mouth and "buzz," it is difficult to determine exactly what media will reach them.

REAL TARGET MARKETING

Because of information clutter and general confusion, direct and interactive communication with students is vital. And communication is bound to attain ever-higher levels of sophistication in the new competitive environment.

For example, a Latin American Studies program may profile likely prospects, and then the admissions office will use available data to locate them. While recruiters now go after students who exhibit an interest in their field, in the future they will seek students in cities that might be generally productive. Schools, of course, will not do this in all disciplines. They will focus on their strongest programs, the ones that clarify and strengthen competitive advantage and brand prominence.

In addition, faculty in priority areas will be asked to help recruit talented students. Eventually, academic programs will have to do what coaches and music teachers have always done: visit prospects' homes and schools and woo them into their programs. Financial aid is but one tool, and most good institutions will have enough aid available to compete. But because the strongest competitive advantage will be a strong relationship, the recruiting process likely will require star faculty to establish relationships with star students long before they complete high school.

BUILDING RELATIONSHIPS WITH HIGH SCHOOLS

Colleges and universities have maintained various kinds of relationships with high schools for a long time. These relationships are likely to grow as competitive advantage becomes a more important factor in student recruiting. Along with adding value to financial aid, these relationships are a comprehensive way to develop "feeder schools" that provide good students consistently over time.

In addition to having certain faculty make coach-like visits to students and schools, there are other ways to cultivate relationships with high schools and their students. Offer selected high schools access to special events. Give them discounts to speaker programs and fine arts performances plus special perks, such as invitations to receptions. Also provide elite campus tours, library privileges (including assistance by special librarians), additional gifted programs, comprehensive college-prep seminars, faculty professional development programs, and new scholarships for specific kinds of students. And, of course, offer "preferred admissions" programs that give fast-track entry to students from selected schools.

Macquarie University in Australia, which does most of the above, enrolls secondary schools in prestigious "associate" relationships—which supports this book's premise that universities worldwide have enhanced programming, better marketing, and a vision for changing the international higher-education marketplace. Australia views itself as a gateway to Asia. Its institutions offer English-language instruction and, once government policies are sorted out, they are likely to engage in innovative student recruiting all over the world. Look out. Other institutions will be doing this kind of recruiting, too—and they will be making the case for seeking opportunities in Asia.

MORE INTENSE COMMUNICATION

More intense communication activity will accompany the targeting of markets such as secondary schools. As universities get better at prioritizing their audiences and assemble talented marketing teams, they are likely to borrow the "creative team" concept from the agency world.

Teams of strategists, designers, writers, and implementers will be formed for each target audience. These teams will design coordinated media activities to attract their targets. These direct and interactive activities will be coordinated with ongoing research activities over time to fine-tune effectiveness. This is happening in many institutions.

For example, teams in some institutions are studying and designing initiatives for the Hispanic market. Elsewhere, teams of marketers and academic program managers are enhancing the role of honors programs in recruiting gifted students and helping new institutes and centers launch their work in the community. The possibilities are almost limitless; the team concept will play a large role in future academic marketing.

NEW STRATEGIES FOR REACHING NEW GENERATIONS

Many marketers have revisited conventional approaches to categorizing markets. While looking at markets in terms of basic demographics (that is, age, income, location, gender, etc.) remains useful, different ways of grouping people can enhance the appeal of the message and the effectiveness of communication.

For example, today there are more mixed-race families, single-parent families, blended families, and so forth. A large number of people in their twenties have returned home to live, and a growing number of grandparents are raising their children's children. The particular characteristics of each group offer deeper insights for marketing than pure demographics. They also affect student recruiting, alumni interests, donor appeals, and perhaps even the expression of competitive advantage.

As mentioned previously, the current generation of high-school students has become hard to reach. They do not read newspapers or follow the news. While they are online often, they might not be online as much as we assume. And when they are online, they are extremely skeptical of pop-up advertising, aggressive come-ons, and blatant recruiting materials. They even discard the DVDs they receive. While very early on they will search your Web site for inside information, they still want to receive printed materials.

To reach them, admissions marketers must find innovative ways first to become visible in their world and then to communicate on their terms. Some institutions place poster ads in shopping centers, send teenagers art posters for their bedrooms, purchase ads at movie theatres, and advertise in high-school papers and athletic programs. Emerging technologies and delivery systems such as RSS (Really Simple Syndication) feeds, podcasts, blogs, text messages, and others facilitate personalized messaging sent directly to computers and cell phones.

WORD-OF-MOUTH AS A TACTIC

There also is a lot of "buzz" in marketing circles about creating "buzz" for products and institutions. The challenge is to organize word-of-mouth campaigns that catch on with targeted markets.

But how do you organize a campaign, launch it, and then know if it is working? Some use Internet chat rooms or streaming discussion boards to generate buzz. They post messages, then ask for responses, and by responding to the responses pass the message along. They eventually "talk the talk" of the target market. You must choose these groups very carefully, and the buzz has to be created by people who have credibility with the group, such as current students. Of course, ethical issues are involved, and the way it is done will be a matter for discussion for a long time.

Another way to create word-of-mouth is to have a group spread the buzz. Give one group of opinion leaders the message and have them pass it along to a list of individuals and groups who pass the message on to others.

The limitations of word-of-mouth are the fundamental lack of control and the need to make messages extremely simple. Your goal can be no more complicated than to obtain peer endorsement for the message, "This is the place to be."

MORE INTERACTIVE TECHNOLOGY

The role of technology is taking new directions, as here, too, the conventional wisdom has been challenged. As mentioned above, students may not be spending as much time on the Internet as we once thought. At the same time, cell-phone technology that incorporates multiple functions is redefining the way people use the device. Future trends remain unclear. Certainly, pure "bells and whistles" features are no longer so impressive, and messages addressed to individuals backfire when they look artificial. But response-driven e-mail messages are likely to remain the basis of successful grassroots marketing efforts.

Many people access university Web sites to obtain information. They expect sites to be comprehensive, yet uncluttered and easy to navigate. They expect to receive responses to questions and to get the "inside story" from "real people," such as current students. As mentioned above, response-driven e-mails work fairly well. Send periodical e-mails to target markets to update them on relevant information. Ask them to respond, and when they do, trigger back a customized message. Ask them to fill out simple surveys; it will add an important research component to the mix.

While you should continue to scrutinize each new piece of technology for marketing potential, be aware that the situation may be settling down and that serious thinking about real communication is taking place once again. The lesson of communication history is that new technology may alter the role of existing technologies, but existing technologies never disappear. Sometimes the old ones assume more prominent roles as their special qualities become better understood and appreciated. Colleges and universities are becoming more sophisticated practitioners in an extremely changing field, and admissions will become ever-closer allies with marketing and communication.

REMEMBER THE CAMPUS VISIT

Human contact, real people talking to real people, undoubtedly will remain the primary persuader. Everything that comes before must prepare students for the experience of the place, and the better the visit the more likely the student will matriculate. It is true now, and it always will be.

But campus visits will become better orchestrated and personalized for specific prospects and families. Visits will emphasize campus services, linking the living experience and the learning experience more than ever. One-on-one encounters between professors and talented prospects will spark interest in mentoring. Personal contact will be emphasized at every turn, simulated early in your communication tactics and writing style, but made real in many ways during the campus visit.

A CHANGING INTERNATIONAL LANDSCAPE

All of this will happen in a rapidly changing world. As the economy moves east and governments cut funds, everything will change—especially student recruiting. Tuition will become an even more important source of income, which, not surprisingly, will motivate interest in casting a wider net for more and better students.

Students will stop yearning to study in the United States because they will have many compelling options all over the world. Universities in Canada, the United Kingdom and the rest of Europe, Australia, Asia, and elsewhere will recruit American undergraduate and graduate students. At the same time, China, India, South American nations, and even South Africa will make greater efforts to educate their most talented students at home. They are already strengthening their universities, and they are rapidly beginning to understand the potential of advancement and marketing.

CHAPTER 10

A BIG FUTURE FOR
ALUMNI RELATIONS

Amid the turmoil and change in higher education, the area of advancement that may emerge as most important is alumni relations. Of course, all areas of advancement are coming front and center, but the alumni base increasingly will be viewed as the key to the institution's future.

Institutions always have considered huge alumni bases instrumental for fund raising and, in some cases, student recruiting. But in a changing, more competitive world, alumni will be essential to perpetuating institutional security. While institutions always will seek students, support, and influence from all market segments, many will make it their business to involve alumni in every way possible and make sure alumni children are willing and able to enroll.

Institutions will comprehensively cultivate lifetime commitments from alumni. Alumni programs no longer can focus on helping grads maintain contact with old friends and hosting enjoyable social and athletic events. Alumni programs must keep all alums connected to the entire institution throughout their own lifetimes and on to future generations.

INFLUENCED BY MARKETING

The marketing mind-set will greatly influence both communication and program development. And while alumni programs have always addressed student recruitment, they are likely to move aggressively into admissions-related activities. Alumni program heads will be expected to engage in reputation building activities and devote as much attention to developing long-term donor loyalty as they do to encouraging participation in the annual fund.

Marketing and communication divisions now spend one-third of their time on admissions, one-third on fund raising and alumni support, and one-third on reputation building (otherwise known as PR). I envision the alumni relations division doing the same in the future as well. It's not that they have not worked in these areas before; they have and they are. But now strategic thinking and program planning will require equally sophisticated and professional work in all areas.

Future alumni relations programs will be influenced by the evolving structures of the marketing and communication divisions. While focused on supporting admissions, fund raising and alumni, and reputation building, the marketing and communication divisions will function more as account executives for schools, colleges, and institution-wide reputation-building programs. They will use all the tools in the communication toolbox to coordinate the identities of individual units with the institution's brand while remaining focused on finding students and money and building reputation. Alumni relations program staff, too, will function more as account executives, helping schools, colleges, and individual academic programs develop comprehensive plans for lifetime alumni involvement.

Because the account-executive approach also is used in fund raising, alumni relations will have to address issues of coordination. And the problem of having a staff person in each area of every school and college will not go away, either! The solution, based on size, history, management culture, leadership style, and other factors, will be different for each institution. But alumni relations ultimately will have to play a stronger role in the big picture. However it is organized, the work of marketing and communication, fund raising, and alumni relations must be integrated. All personnel will have to function as planners and account executives charged with developing resources, finding the right students, and building reputation where it counts.

INTERNATIONAL IMPLICATIONS

Because U.S. colleges and universities have been involved in alumni relations for a long time, they have strong programs and a long history to build on. Few institutions in other countries can say the same.

Many countries view higher education as an entitlement for students, paid for by large taxes. Until recently, the concept that students in these countries might "owe back" to the institution did not exist, and it may take a while for this attitude to change. Nonetheless, many countries are quickly and aggressively gearing up alumni programs with no lack of professional expertise. Advancement has become truly international of late; professional meetings are now places to exchange ideas, not tutorials by American practitioners. While conditions are different in each country, the same dynamic is at play all over the world: Everybody is looking to alumni bases for security.

As the international marketplace changes, U.S. institutions will be cultivating their international alumni more aggressively. Foreign institutions will be looking for more money and students in the United States and vice versa. Because both U.S. and overseas institutions will be contacting wealthy people all over the world, comprehensive international alumni programs that help U.S. institutions find students and money in target market countries will expand.

Significantly, governments that had sent students to the United States in the past think differently now. As economic prosperity and growth shift eastward, foreign countries are improving their institutions, both to keep talented students at home and to attract more Americans.

SOCIAL ROLE OF ALUMNI RELATIONS

The traditional role of alumni relations will be no less important. While emphasizing other areas of activity, alumni relations must continue to facilitate the community building and bonding of alumni who were socially active campus leaders. This group must be inspired and mobilized to develop the other programs. Thus programs built around athletics will continue to thrive, as will social events that celebrate individual achievement. Travel programs also will continue. And current volunteers will be pressed into even greater service.

Integrated marketing and communication must inspire former students to assume larger roles. Once the institution has clarified its brand in terms of competitive advantage and developed a message-on-a-page that summarizes its strengths and identity, the marketing and communication staff can formulate a plan for taking this message, in an inspirational context, to alumni-organization opinion leaders. When leadership "walks the talk" of a new and exciting vision for alumni, the groundwork exists for expanding the base and moving ahead.

ALUMNI FUND RAISING

Expanding activities will not reduce the importance of alumni in fund raising. On the contrary, it will reinforce and expand it.

Certainly, the annual fund will become more important than ever. Alumni programs will be tied tightly to advancing the institution's mission and vision, as supported by the message-on-a-page. Communication will reinforce the university's desire to play a larger role in the lives of alumni families. Appeals will be based as much on continuing service to alumni as on building a better university.

Maintaining donor loyalty will remain a challenge. Loyalty goes far beyond contributing to the annual fund. With so many entities and causes competing for major contributions, institutions cannot take donor loyalty for granted. The alumni program, therefore, must play a strong role in retaining major donors who happen to be alumni. Alumni programs that focus on individuals should be very attractive to these donors.

GREATER ROLE IN ADMISSIONS

While alumni programs always have been concerned with building legacies, admissions offices believe alumni associations are more likely to apply pressure to admit unqualified students than to find talented ones.

Traditionally, U.S. alumni organizations have supplied alumni for high-school college nights, organized send-off parties for local freshman, and involved the dean of admissions or staff in various other ways. The future likely will see more thorough alumni involvement.

First, willing and able alumni will be better trained to serve as university representatives. Alumni will be asked to aid more systematically in the search for highly qualified students in specific academic areas and to formulate strategies for recruiting them. Alumni will receive additional professional support for their work, and they will be expected to get other alumni involved in the endeavor. Alumni activity will become their avocation, and they will receive rewards and recognition for their service.

Second, alumni families will receive greater support in "developing" alumni legacies. Along with sending them information about admission requirements early on, alumni organizations will counsel the families and help their children prepare.

At many institutions, a huge alumni base creates a diverse marketplace for students. For example, satisfied minority students can be very effective at recruiting, especially when given professional assistance. Of course, they understand it is to their advantage to build the minority population of their alma mater. Likewise, past honor students can be highly motivated recruiters of future honor students, especially if they had a great experience and remain involved in honors program issues and programming.

In the future, more alumni club programs will spread the word about the university's strengths and inspire word-of-mouth support for student recruiting. Constant communication will make alumni regard the institution as part of the culture, fill them with action-oriented pride, and inspire them to talk it up with professional colleagues and friends.

REPUTATION-BUILDING ROLE

Alumni who play a greater role in developing the message at the outset will be asked to spread the word actively. The message-on-a-page

lets everyone who communicates the university, both professionals and volunteers, speak with a single voice about what makes the
place special.

Developing the brand can be a bonding process for all key constituents, including alumni. A series of questions discussed at meetings
can get groups to agree on the central messages. These meetings can
occupy the better part of a day, or at least half a day. Alumni clubs can
hold them, as can national boards and groups of leaders. Afterwards,
facilitators can compile each group's answers into a composite that
eventually can be refined into the message-on-a-page.

Experience indicates how compatible these groups can be, even
groups of trustees, university leaders, staff, academic deans and
administrators, students, and alumni. It is seldom difficult to create a
composite message from their collective ideas. And the process itself
achieves a buy-in that spurs willingness to get out and tell the story.

Arm alumni groups with the message-on-a-page, or something
similar, and train them to spread the word. Training, too, can be fun
and engaging, giving opportunities to offer how-to suggestions in
small-group brainstorming sessions. The professional term for this
activity is "word-of-mouth" communication, and it is a hot topic in
marketing today. The strategy is first to shape the message and then
tell communicators where to go and how to present it.

In the electronic version of word-of-mouth communication,
alumni log into a suitable Internet chat room, or threaded discussion,
and create "buzz" around the institution's central message. Alumni
stay in the conversation long enough to get the buzz going. This type
of word-of-mouth communication can reach prospective students,
fellow alumni, and special-interest groups that could include prospective parents.

Of course, while it is difficult to measure the effectiveness of word-of-mouth, staying closely involved in the projects will enable you to sense what is and is not working. And organized as suggested above, groups can return for debriefings. The key is to make the training fun, and then follow up later.

Alumni also can participate in other kinds of communications, that is, speaking to key groups, representing the university at conferences, even handling some kinds of media relations. However, you need to coordinate these activities carefully with the university office of communications.

In media relations it is important to speak with a single voice, even when several people are doing the speaking. Nothing clutters the information environment more than different individuals making conflicting statements to the news media. Well-intentioned alumni create such clutter and in the end do more harm than good.

However, the right alumnus approaching the right reporter can yield good results. It is possible to recruit appropriate alumni to help with specific media-relations initiatives and work closely with the office of communications on any project. Some offices of communication may quarrel with this, but the news media prefer talking to "real people" and do not consider media relations professionals to be among them. Using well-briefed alumni helps send the message, and it gives the right alumni something important to do.

CONTINUING EDUCATION

Lifelong learning is becoming important for many reasons, and it is likely to become a larger part of alumni programs in the future. Most public institutions—and many private ones—

believe that educating adults in their communities is part of their mission. But in the past, however, other institutions focused on traditional-aged students did not view adult education as a core business.

There are compelling reasons for alumni relations to embrace continuing education. Most notably, continuing education provides opportunities to provide lifelong services to those traditional students and their families, including updates in their career areas, retraining for new careers, general enrichment, education on personal and family issues, and other services. These services can be associated with special events, lectures, performances, retreats, travel-study tours, and more. And it all establishes and prolongs a bond with obvious fund-raising and student-recruitment implications.

But this will require a close working relationship between alumni relations and the continuing education division of the university. It can involve little more than customizing the communication about existing continuing-education offerings, or it may mean that you have to develop new programs. Many universities offer summer-education programs and travel-study opportunities for alumni families. But depending on the size and location of your alumni base, you may have to organize many new seminars and lecture programs.

If you do not already have them, consider offering seminars on re-evaluating careers, developing leadership potential, or dealing with the college-selection process. Distinguished lecturer series can be popular, as well as conferences on hot topics or with new authors. Fruitful collaboration with continuing education professionals can evolve over time. Ultimately, alumni relations work is an exercise that brings the whole university to the alumni for a lifetime.

SPECIAL INTEREST GROUPS

Creating special interest groups, or "SIGs," is another way to broaden the base, but it involves careful planning and organization. Choosing the right interests and staffing the meetings are not easy, but the concept is sound, especially in light of your future needs.

Before you can serve alumni who were absorbed in special interests while on campus, you have to figure out how to reach them. Begin with groups that are computer- or Internet-related, or groups involved in music or art. Then find committed volunteer alumni leaders for each group, and provide them with training and support. How you organize and delegate really matters.

Use a survey to identify interest areas, and then find leaders for each interest area; contact survey respondents who expressed that particular interest. Or send mailings to all, and ask them to select. Groups can be formed within each alumni club or at the university. Groups can meet on the Internet, via teleconferences, at alumni club sites, or on campus; use various combinations. Involving a university resource—that is, an expert faculty member, a staff member with special expertise, etc.—with each group will give them substance and credibility. Highly regarded alumni with appropriate credentials can lead SIGs as well. The key is to give many people a chance to get involved.

USE OF TECHNOLOGY

Technology is changing everything, and successful alumni programs will have to make major use of it. The overall program must look technology-savvy but still focus on connecting real people.

Of course, every alumni association must put its directory online. This invaluable resource keeps people connected with the university as they search for each other. And Web sites do a much better job of establishing that connection than the old printed directories.

Web sites also can provide much more information in a timely fashion. This includes news about campus events and information about jobs and career opportunities. Web sites enable alumni to find help within the university, publicize individual club projects and activities, and provide links to other relevant sites. A properly designed and maintained Web site can be a one-stop information resource and gateway to the rest of the world.

The Web site can host chat rooms and threaded discussions, as well as the SIGs described above. Home page links can access descriptions of chat room topics and expert resources, as well as instructions for entering the discussion. Joining chat rooms might be free, but you defray costs by charging for related activities and events.

Of course, e-mail newsletters will remain critical components of the electronic mix. E-newsletters are inexpensive ways to transmit information regularly to most alumni. The cost of postage deters most organizations from developing relationships with international alumni. Mailing the alumni magazine alone is extremely expensive. The Internet and e-mail are a boon for international alumni programs. While not everyone is online, e-mail now reaches most educated people and makes it easier to update addresses.

WORKING WITH ACADEMIC DEPARTMENTS AND SCHOOLS

Alumni associations have had problems working with academic departments and schools in the past, and establishing good relations with them will not be quick and easy. But academics are going to have to get more involved in all areas of advancement if they want their programs to compete and, in many cases, survive.

To compete for good students, academic departments will have to establish relationships with them before they arrive. If they want to attract more money and build donor loyalty, they will have to give donors meaningful connections to their work. Further, if they want to build their department's reputation, they will have to stop pushing the office of communications to place non-news stories in the media and get involved in the development and implementation of meaningful strategic plans. And if they want lifelong commitments from their alumni, they will have to offer them continuing, meaningful connections.

All of this involves taking time away from what they perceive as their core business, teaching and research, to engage in activities that up to now they considered someone else's job. But someone else's job is going to be performing the marketing research, developing the plans, coordinating the message, and designing the programs. Academics often are the only ones who can deliver the goods in a credible way. Indeed, they must begin to see total higher education as their core business, and they must broaden their job description to include advancing that business.

Establishing this cooperative environment will take time and patience. Academics always suspect that central administration is trying to take away their independence. "Why don't they let us alone?" "Let them do their jobs, and we'll do ours." The only way to change this attitude will be with good old-fashioned relationship building, including one-on-one communication that builds trust and shared vision.

Advancement should approach academics with the attitude, "I hear you do great things. I am here to learn more about what you do." Then later, "I think we can help you reach your goals and enhance your individual brand identity." Still later, "Let's together develop a comprehensive strategic plan that maintains your identity, advances your goals, and still ties into the university's identity and overall goals." And finally, "Here is what our staff can do to implement this plan. Will you do your part to make it work?"

Eventually, everybody will understand clearly where the prospective students are and what it will take to get them, where the money is and what it will take to get it, and what it will take to build an academic reputation in an information-cluttered world.

MARKETING STRATEGIES

Marketing and communication and alumni relations have a long and interesting road ahead. The expectations of alumni relations will broaden and deepen significantly, and marketing and communication will bring all its strategic thinking and tools to the task.

Marketing and communication will pay more attention to "lifecycle" marketing, studying the stages people go through as they get older and customizing programming and communications to meet their needs.

Marketing and communication will bring to bear the new "lifestyle groupings" discussed previously. It is not just the younger generations that think differently; older generations develop different common interests and cluster into different groups as they age.

In terms of direct and interactive communication, fewer, better-targeted mass mailings will be the way of the future. And we will work much harder to obtain feedback. Some attempts to obtain feedback will be built into the communication process itself; others will require additional research.

Research will be more segmented, as well. Up to now, we have viewed alumni as a single group. Now we view alumni as comprising different age groups with different family roles and special interests. We will have to study each group separately to develop effective programs.

We will place increased importance on the garments we sell to alumni, especially on their designs and logos. Clothing has become a personal witness to their wearer's support and a powerful way to extend brand reach. Alumni associations, together with marketing and communication operations, will work closely with the bookstore and other retail outlets to design garments that both sell and build the power of the brand.

Of course, alumni events will be seen not merely as social gatherings but as opportunities to communicate messages printed in the invitation to target groups, reinforce the brand during events themselves and with associated materials, deliver important messages to captive target markets, and receive helpful feedback from important constituencies. Do not waste time and money just to throw a party. Throw one that communicates and inspires as well.

ULTIMATE BRANDING

Except for its students, an institution's alumni are the best people to tell its story to the world. After making a huge investment in the place, alumni maintain a lifetime association with it. Can there be better conditions for marketing?

Alumni are in many ways walking billboards—literally so when they wear garments that proudly display the school logo. In the changing higher education landscape ahead, we must mobilize this huge, critically important mass to make sure the institution fulfills its mission to educate leaders who will change the world once again. The kinds of alumni program that will do this either are now or will soon become vital parts of every academic institution in the world. This is a truly international trend.

CHAPTER 11

SEARCHING FOR MORE REVENUE

The need to find new sources of revenue and maximize old sources is the most obvious consequence of government cutbacks. Clearly, public and private institutions will become more alike: Public institutions will need to increase revenue from tuition and fund raising, while privates will have to find additional sources of public funding.

THE CHANGING PUBLIC INSTITUTION

Cutbacks are occurring all over the world and in most U.S. states. Along with finding new ways to boost income from tuition, publics will have to take advantage of every aspect of private philanthropy. Fund raisers will broaden their areas of solicitation to include program sponsorships, and the university itself will take a harder look at which programs make money. Some public universities will consider becoming private. The revenue-producing potential of programs, combined with the fundraising potential of an enormous alumni base, can create compelling urges to be free of government money and government control.

EFFECT ON PROGRAM DEVELOPMENT

The search for revenue from program development can have consequences for both public and private institutions. Some academic programs make money and some do not. Programs like business and communications attract enough students to more than pay for themselves, but programs such as music and art are costly because they require so much one-on-one interaction, small-group teaching, and coaching. The overall budget, however, usually balances out because the more lucrative programs underwrite the others.

In the search for revenue, however, the programs that lose out may be those that form the foundation of academic institutions—the humanities, social sciences, physical sciences, and fine arts. As revenue considerations motivate institutions to expand and add professional programs that meet momentary marketplace needs, the academy can become more vocation-oriented and less a center of teaching and research.

A FINANCIAL STALEMATE

Many private institutions, especially the smaller ones, have a dilemma. In the face of annual budgeting, the potential for new revenue is limited. Because alumni bases are limited, increases from fund raising may be modest. It is becoming increasingly difficult for small institutions to raise tuition significantly because, when they do, they must offset the increase with significant financial aid. Many small privates have assumed long-term debt to fund the facilities and services they need to remain competitive, and servicing that debt takes a larger bite out of the annual operations budget. And the high costs of maintaining the physical plant, library resources, computer technology, aging scientific equipment, and faculty salaries make the financial picture look bleak. Large endowments do not help because large deficits quickly deplete them. In any event, most institutions can use only a small percentage of their annual earnings for operations.

This dilemma forces private institutions to make difficult cost-cutting decisions—canceling programs, cutting staff, reducing plant maintenance, and taking other measures that diminish quality. And when private institutions lose their quality, they lose much of their reason to exist.

Like public institutions, private institutions will seek additional public funding—financial aid, research support, and funds for special programs—from the federal government, state government, even their city.

In fact, private institutions could make the case that they are important enough to the city to justify substantial support. After all, they contribute to overall economic development, attract businesses and talent, educate the workforce, provide employment, and offer cultural enrichment. Private institutions are as critical to the city's vitality as the museums, the performing arts, and other entities that already benefit from tax revenue. Especially in the absence of a local public institution, privates may be very willing to become more public. Some might even adopt their city's name.

CORPORATE SPONSORSHIPS AND PARTNERSHIPS

Both publics and privates will be looking for more and different sponsorships. Just as the names of donors now appear on buildings, donor names will soon be associated with much smaller programs, with institutions permitting a larger measure of corporate involvement in the planning and implementation of the programs as a condition of that support. Of course, all of this goes on now, but the future will bring increased efforts to procure support in many more program areas.

IN-KIND GIFTS AND LOANS

In-kind gifts and loans are not new, but, like sponsorships, institutions will put more emphasis on seeking them, especially in the area of technology. Keeping up with technological developments will be so costly that many institutions will forge partnerships with corporations that will supply new technology on a regular basis. Deals with outside organizations to build and operate housing and other businesses on or near campus will expand as well.

WHAT ABOUT FOUNDATIONS?

Foundations will be more important than ever, but every foundation is different and has different goals. Some institutions rely on local foundations for regular help. But many of these arrangements will change, too. Every imaginable charity already can make a compelling case for support, and that will intensify. Some foundations tackle special projects and defer other giving for a prolonged period of time—great when you are the special project but not so great when you are not.

For example, in one city each of three foundations had a special-interest museum. Each museum underwent a huge expansion, calling upon the resources of the others to finance the expansions. Each museum took its turn, and during that period the three foundations made much less money available for other projects and causes, including universities.

In some cases, organizations will have to get into a foundation's "queue" and wait their turn for funding. Societal changes, especially revolutionary changes in education, will have foundations swamped with requests, each delivered with pressure from somewhere and a strong sense of urgency. Foundation gifts cannot be taken for granted, and the competition for them will become even more demanding and time-consuming.

A NEW DAY FOR FUND RAISING

All of the above activities, along with new pressures to expand them, will alter the job descriptions and day-to-day work of fund raisers. The need to find staff somewhere in the institution to formulate plans for seeking specific sponsorships, partnerships, and in-kind donations will change fund raisers' lives. Corporate fund raising, as it now exists in most institutions, undoubtedly will expand. In smaller institutions where it may not exist at all, corporate fund raising may suddenly become a key concern.

GROWING DONOR FATIGUE

Donor fatigue will strike in environments where aggressive fund raising has existed for some time—very much in the United States, much less in nations where fund raising is relatively new. But foreign institutions can assume that the competitive international market sooner or later will affect their donors in the same way.

In the wake of one intense campaign after another, many donors get that I've-been-here-before look. I believe it will be a challenge to keep them interested, and after three or four campaigns it will be close to impossible. Not all fund raisers agree. They feel that campaign mode is the future of the profession. But a lot of evidence indicates that in the future, real complications will arise if we go on doing things as we have in the past.

MAINTAINING DONOR LOYALTY

Donor loyalty will be a big issue, especially given the danger of wearing out people through repeated campaigns. Donors face both annual funds and campaigns in every facet of their community life. All the boards they serve on—human services boards, cultural boards, performing arts boards, museum boards, hospital boards—expect board of trustee commitment and participation in annual funds and regular campaigns. Plus, these people often serve on the boards of more than one academic institution, perhaps a university and a private K-12 school. One trustee in the Southwest is a member of a university board, chairs the board of another college, and contributes money to both.

FUTURE OF CAMPAIGNS

For the most part, current fund-raising practices still work, and you should pursue them as long as they do. In one form or another, they all will be used in the future. But because institutions can expect donor loyalty to fade and donor fatigue to set in, prudent, forward-thinking professionals will plan alternative activities. No longer can institutions assume that their donors' universities will remain their primary philanthropic interest throughout their lives.

Each campaign will need to have a new and interesting twist. Some institutions will come up with a new word to replace "campaign," others will vary time frames, and all will search for meaningful new campaign activities and forms of recognition.

Most major donors have appeared already on every recognition list, received every certificate, and been honored at every imaginable dinner. Now what? More of the same? Or can you give them something more?

GIFT CLUBS AND RECOGNITIONS

Raising donors to successively higher giving levels is a successful practice that will continue in some form. But activities associated with the gift clubs and the recognition at the end of campaigns will have to be much more meaningful than certificates or paperweights. Ego is a factor, and donors do like to read their names on the right list, see their picture in newsletters, and get recognized at dinners. But when that wears thin, the question becomes, "What is really meaningful to this person?" The answer will be critical and different for each donor. A simple honor may work for one person, while another donor is just happy to be involved in an exciting, meaningful project. The simple honor might work at first, but you will need a more complicated plan for long-term cultivation.

NEW WAYS TO ORGANIZE

Traditional ways of organizing fund-raising activities are likely to change too. Today, assigning some staff to the annual fund while others call on major donors and still others work on deferred giving is standard practice. While these categories of giving may remain, the fund raisers themselves will consider many new ways to organize their work. For example, they may organize regionally, with each region handling all forms of fund raising. Or they may organize around academic areas. Or, more radically, they may organize around donor interest areas.

As in alumni relations, start thinking about donor cultivation in terms of special interests. What is it about the university that really engages them, and how can they get meaningfully involved? You can cluster donors around a number of interest areas, e.g., business leadership, human welfare issues, visual arts, performing arts, technology, etc. Assign an advancement staff member to partner with an academic staff or faculty member to coordinate "experiences" and "involvements" in each area and to handle annual giving, major gifts, deferred planning, or campaign contacts at the appropriate time.

ACADEMIC PROGRAM INVOLVEMENT

Now we come to the most difficult yet potentially important factor in future success: academic programs. Just as they recruit students and plan reputation building initiatives, academics need to get more involved in developing the loyalty essential for gift cultivation.

This means more than merely making fund-raising calls with development officers. Rather, it includes academics helping development officers conceive of reasonable and meaningful ways to get donors involved. You might have to modify the policy of keeping donors away from program areas they fund. Of course, there has to be a clear understanding about matters such as who has authority over the final program, political agendas, and control; donors will have to be reasonable about that. But if donors have a passion for a subject, keeping them involved cultivates loyalty.

Invite donors to faculty meetings. Meetings planned with the donors' presence in mind can review research, consider new courses, discuss student achievements, etc. Ask donors to audit classes or speak at classes in areas where they have expertise. Invite them to participate in panel discussions, witness others, and attend special "insider" guest lectures. Or ask them to departmental social events and to formal and informal meetings with students. These activities keep donors involved without giving them control or bending to their political ideology.

Of course, these activities will not just happen; someone has to coordinate them. What it will take is a partnership between the development office and the academic department involving the cooperation and participation of all faculty members. But the social changes that will alter our industry's competitive realities will require faculty to become more involved in all aspects of admissions and advancement. We will have to introduce this kind of outside-the-box thinking gradually and make participation as easy and rewarding as possible.

BECOMING PART OF THE VISION

The key concept is "passion factor." The challenge is to position all constituents, but most importantly donors, so that they can share the vision. That means shaping the vision whenever planning is participatory, whether at the department, school, or institutional level. It means helping to implement it, especially when implementation is appropriate to the participants' expertise and circumstances. It means, when necessary, articulating the passion on behalf of the program or institution. And it means making constituents feel that they are living the passion in their own lives.

The academic development officer of the future will need all the leadership qualities described in Chapter 2. To inspire others with "passion for the business," development officers will have to feel it themselves.

This is a complex endeavor with many facets; outsiders often are surprised at just how complicated it is. Often they say, "It must be easy to market a university, certainly easier than marketing my company." Or, "It can't be difficult to raise money for that place." But because academic institutions are more like small cities than companies, because it is difficult for institutions to even define their products, because it takes special people to work with academics, and because academic institutions are highly politicized entities that demand a combination of persistence and patience, marketing and raising money is endlessly complex and challenging.

Academic institutions need advancement professionals who have a passion for the business and a lifetime commitment to it. Development officers who believe they can raise money for any organization and can move easily among hospitals, charities, and education institutions need not apply. Too many development offices have swinging doors, with people coming and going. Where this is the case, it will have to change. This work is not easy. Advancement professionals must understand and appreciate what this exciting world of "higher" education is all about, empathize with living the life of the mind, esteem those who devote their lives to teaching and research, and completely comprehend why it is necessary to possess passion to inspire passion.

The future will be extremely bright for the right people, as academic institutions will need us more than ever. But those folks with "vocational wanderlust" should go elsewhere. We have too much important work to do.

CHAPTER 12

DEALING WITH CHANGE

Universities typically are slow to change. As large, personnel-heavy organizations with more or less decentralized management and an extreme diversity of lifestyles and attitudes, they generally focus more on keeping up with change in academic fields than on changing the institution itself. External people view them as antiquated organizations that waste resources and do not belong to the real world.

In many ways, the opposite is true now and will become truer in the years ahead. Many predict a sea change in higher education brought on mainly by government cutbacks but also by a changing international marketplace for students and growing economic opportunities for graduates in different parts of the world. To adapt quickly and become competitive, institutions will be forced to recruit more entrepreneurial leadership. In short, institutions will change or they will perish.

ATTITUDES OF ACADEMIC DEANS

Most deans today are expected to perform the same roles as presidents: raise money, recruit students, motivate and inspire staff and faculty, manage budgets efficiently, elevate their school's reputation and prestige. Given these expectations, deans compete with each other for resources and find it difficult to eagerly support activities that promote the institution's common good—especially if promoting the common good involves sacrificing resources.

This is understandable. It is easy to sympathize with deans who believe that, given sufficient resources, they could raise the reputation of the entire school. But it does not actually work that way. In this changing competitive world, the institution itself must possess a clear, differentiated identity, and the schools and colleges must help establish it. An institution's limited visibility and prestige becomes a ceiling that must be raised before the schools and colleges within can prosper. Otherwise, they are more limited than they realize, and to think otherwise is self-deception.

We must convince academic deans that the advancement professions exist to help them succeed. It must become one of our primary objectives. We have to help them establish their own identities and produce materials that underscore their identities. Schools of business must look businesslike, engineering must look high-tech, fine arts must look cutting edge. However, we also must make sure school materials resemble institution-wide materials. This activates a branding program that will raise that ceiling, connecting the schools and the institution emotionally and effectively to market targets.

OTHER ACADEMIC ATTITUDES

There is much tradition associated with the academy. Many academics work hard to qualify for the "academic life." Outsiders might consider academic life unrealistic, but it is important for society to enable some people to "live a subject matter" and immerse themselves in the search for truth. Living in the world of ideas produces inspired teaching and breakthrough discoveries. Academic life may seem unrealistic, but it produces some of the most interesting and compelling people on earth.

Yet when it comes to some kinds of change, academics by nature resist. While they are usually on the cutting edge of change in their fields, they resist changes elsewhere because they are not focusing on other things around them. When changes are put into context and explained in academic terms, academics embrace them. They just love their lifestyle and want to be sure that those who are asking them to change understand what the academic life is all about.

With deans, make sure the teacher-scholar knows you understand what he or she does, that you respect and admire it, and that your number one job is to advance it. Portray institutional change as necessary to fully advance their work. It takes time and effort to communicate this to academics, who will insist on substantive arguments and reassurance that their cherished community of living and learning will be preserved. None of the changes proposed here will threaten this at all. In fact, the changes are to make the adjustments necessary to ensure the life of the mind survives in a complex future.

PRESIDENTS AND CHANGE

Advancement people ask me how they can make their presidents understand how rapidly conditions are changing and exactly what they are going to have to do to succeed in the coming years. Presidents who have climbed a traditional academic and scholarly ladder still believe their world is stable and secure. They are scholars and administrators, not entrepreneurial visionaries. Some presidents maintain that governments eventually will come to their senses and reinstate their support, and that in the long run their prestige as research institutions will keep the students and money coming. They believe that everything cycles and that declining enrollments will come back when the economy or demographics improve.

I have argued that government cutbacks reflect a shift in ideology related to who should pay for education and that this, coupled with shifts in the world economy, has altered the student marketplace and all the rules of fund raising. Most of all, it has sparked a need for a new breed of change-oriented leaders who are more akin to corporate leaders than past administrators but also driven by love of the academic world and its special role in life and civilization.

INDIVIDUAL RESISTANCE TO CHANGE

Even we advocates for change are sometimes disappointingly resistant. In introspective moments, we admit it. We may concede that change is necessary but find it so frightening that we find ways in our daily behavior to resist it. In *Leading Change* (Harvard Business School Press, 1996), John P. Kotter of the Harvard Business School provides insight about both resisting change and overcoming that resistance.

Facts rarely change behavior. Many people who know the facts about smoking continue to smoke. Others, unhappy with their weight, continue to overeat. And people in the academic life may know the world is changing but prefer to pretend otherwise, denying the facts and keeping their current world view intact.

Others see the changes coming but struggle to resist them. But some change is inevitable, and programs and individuals that oppose it are doomed to failure. Many in marketing and communication, for example, still believe information offices should just send out information as it comes to them. They feel they are gatekeepers of the flow of information and, as trained journalists, it is not their job to shape brand identity and "market" reputation-defining stories to specific audiences. For them, a desire to preserve professional practice prompts them to resist and even undermine the new emphasis on marketing communication.

But many changes have come about already because the forces of competition have required them. They are inevitable, and when fully explained, they can be fully accepted.

Here is an example that academics can understand: Marketing is a way of thinking, not commercializing, and as such meets the needs of prospective students. But the process only begins there. It, along with the entire collegiate experience, awakens needs students never knew they had. Explained this way, even opponents can understand and embrace changing the way we present education to the world. The key is to see the big picture and understand its context. But backsliding is always a possibility, because following old ways is easier and, at least in the present, more comfortable.

Some think organizational structures should be changed immediately. But experience has taught me that if you change the structure of the operation around new guidelines, personnel will go on as they did before. Their behavior changes little, often not at all, even when it involves developing a new plan of action.

This is yet another reason why some strategic plans and marketing plans are never implemented. Most plans are too detailed and ignore the realities of daily demands. People spend months developing plans but never actually change what they do every day. Years later someone will say, "We need to develop a marketing plan." And someone else will say, "We did one several years ago. It's over there on the shelf."

SEEING THE BIG PICTURE

Much of the material in this book derives from domestic and international campus visits, many advancement operations assessments, numerous staff and faculty group discussions, and countless professional-development seminars. Reflecting on those experiences reinforces my belief that the change process begins only when people see the big picture. While scholars may believe the so-called "big picture people" lack facts and data, facts and data do not motivate most change. When people see change emotionally in the context of the big picture—that is, what is happening in the world, alterations of government realities, shifts in the economy, dramatic changes in student behavior patterns—they are convinced that change is necessary.

EMOTIONAL DIMENSIONS OF CHANGE

Harvard's Kotter discusses how change must speak to feelings. Advocates of change must influence emotion, not just thoughts. And emotional persuasion has both psychological and spiritual dimensions. It speaks to a person's life orientation and how change can make life more exciting. Emotional persuasion does not rely on dangerous facts that force an undesired, difficult-to-achieve change in behavior. Rather, it says, change this way and your whole life will take on new, inspired meaning. It will be exciting to be a part of a whole new day. You will feel great if you do.

HOW TO LEAD CHANGE

Contrary to conventional wisdom, it can be easier to make major changes than small ones. Institutions that have tried making incremental changes have failed. They are often more successful when a new president announces that it is a whole new ballgame and invites people to come along for a wonderful adventure. Suddenly, there is a sense that the institution is finally "stepping out." Staff start overlooking the little problems and feel the excitement that accompanies new behaviors and activities.

Of course, institutional change has to be tied to the traditions and cultural traits of academic life. If change is emotionally motivated, the payoff has to be felt in daily campus life. You have to articulate institutional values, render traditions compatible with the change, and make mission and vision the rallying cry for forward movement. Leaders must orchestrate a total institutional plan aimed at emotional and, therefore, lifestyle satisfaction—not sacrifice and hardship.

CREATING CHANGE

Kotter posits eight steps for creating change. Although developed for the corporate world, they adapt well to the academy:

1. **Create a sense of urgency.** The need for change in the academy is urgent. Leadership teams must determine how social-change factors affect them and what kind of plan will inspire people emotionally.

2. **Form a guiding coalition.** The organization needs to install a group of leaders to orchestrate a plan successfully. In academia, this often begins with a "champion" for marketing who can explain to the academics how marketing can help institutions become more effective.

3. **Clarify vision and strategy.** The vision must be simple and compelling, not the usual pages of academic verbiage that make universities all sound alike. Rather, vision statements must differentiate the institution from its competitors and clearly express its competitive advantage. The strategy must outline actions essential for hitting a few simple market targets that, if achieved, will fulfill the mission.

4. **Communicate the vision.** Easier said than done. Many important, institution-defining messages get lost in information clutter. The challenge is to communicate the vision constantly with clarity, intensity, and a targeted focus. When you are tired of hearing it, internal and external people are just beginning to pay attention.

5. **Empower broad-based action.** The key words are "empower" and "broad-based." "Empower" means that key leaders inside the organization have been authorized to take major action. "Broad-based" means that this action must take place throughout the entire organization, not just at the top.

6. **Create short-term wins.** This is critically important. So many grand visions are long term by their nature and can run out of emotional steam somewhere along the way. Strategic thinking requires shorter-term achievement moments that serve as periodical opportunities for celebrations and rewards.

7. **Consolidate gains.** In academia this means showing how gains in specific areas benefit all, especially when strategically designed to

do so. But leadership has to clearly explain and constantly reinforce this message.

8. **Anchor changes in the culture.** This is a point well worth repeating, especially in the context of academic institutions. Sweeping change will have to be seen as necessary for preserving the essential features of the academic lifestyle, the magic of teaching, and the discovery of knowledge. This may sound like a paradox—change to preserve tradition—but it is not.

Change is not easy, for institutions or for individuals. But it will be forced upon us by sweeping changes in government support, changing international student markets, and a changing world economy. Many anticipate a rapid change in our industry. It will be difficult for institutions that have been slow to change and for leaders untrained as entrepreneurs. It will go against the human impulse to resist change even when there is good reason for it.

But the leaders we need will emerge, and they will succeed if they call for change in the context of the big picture and realize that sweeping, emotion-based change will be easier than gradual change. These people must come from inside education, because they will have to have a burning passion for the business and an unstoppable drive to succeed.

CHAPTER 13

LEARNING TO LOVE THE POLITICS

At this time of sea change in higher education, academic advancement people will be thrust into front-and-center roles around the world. To take on the challenge, people in marketing, fund raising, alumni relations, and also admissions will have to be more involved with institutional politics than ever before. To be effective—and to climb the ladder of professional success—they will have to learn both how to work the political system and how to like it.

GETTING PAST HATE

Most advancement positions require specific expertise and talent. Advancement professionals produce special events, market alumni programs, perform various kinds of research, cultivate relationships, write copy, design materials, and take on an array of other professional tasks. When institutional politics get in the way by altering decisions, dictating designs, slowing progress on projects, or just failing to appreciate their expertise, professionals get frustrated and typically say, "I hate the politics. Just let me alone to do my work."

This attitude is fine for people who want to become the best writer who ever lived or the best designer or the best events manager. But those who aspire to management positions in academic institutions will have to modify that view and acquire a high degree of political skill. Managers do an immense amount of political strategizing. And they succeed only if they learn to like the politics and devote a large part of their workday to it. In fact, most successful top executives say, "Yes, I can do the politics. Yes, I can be successful. And yes, I am actually learning to like it!"

EXPLAIN WHAT YOU ARE DOING

CBS news anchor Bob Schieffer once told me that serious news people should do a better job of getting out and telling people what they are trying to do. He was making the point that doing something important is not enough. To make people understand what you are doing, you need to explain exactly what you are trying to do. Delivering quality products or services is but one professional function; a separate function is explaining what you are trying to do and why it is important. It is called marketing, and it is what managers in academic institutions do: market what the institution is trying to do. Managers do the explaining, while the experts deal with the difficult issues that surface in the process.

MY BOSS NEEDS TO HEAR THIS

People attending advancement or marketing workshops for professional development often say, "This stuff is great, but my bosses need to hear it. I am now going back to a bunch of people who just don't get it! What will I do?" They feel they don't receive sufficient support, and that it takes far too long to get things approved and moving. They are trapped at their desks without a clue about how to get the support they need to do the job they do so well.

Good work must be accompanied by an aggressive action plan for telling people what you are trying to do. Yes, this ought to be in the job description of the area manager, but individuals can do a lot on their own if they think strategically and develop a bit of savvy. Indeed, now that advancement is becoming more central to everything, the political dimensions of gaining internal support are more important than ever.

WHAT ACADEMICS THINK ABOUT ADVANCEMENT

It is dangerous and unfair to make generalizations about what entire categories of people think. Deans do not all think alike (although it sometimes seems they do). But because few academics inhabit environments where they learn much about advancement, academics do not consider advancement people professional practitioners, like lawyers or doctors, but staff whose job is to serve them. Some advancement people ask for money. Others write (but write what they are told to write). Or design (but design what they are told to design). Still others organize events. But academics rate advancement professionals more by how well they respond to their demands than on their professional talents.

Many who have made their lives in the academy are not aware that advancement also involves strategic thinking and planning, skillful research, knowledge of the media business, cutting-edge design, and an incredible abundance of individual talent. Appreciation for the higher-level, professional dimensions of our field has to be marketed internally, and it has to be marketed every day. Otherwise, advancement professionals, and what they do, will be taken for granted. It is just that simple.

As mentioned in Chapter 12, deans and program heads often are expected to perform many of the same functions as the president. They are expected to raise money, find students, and build the reputation of their schools. Sadly, deans and program heads sometimes fancy themselves experts in these areas and fail to consult with the advancement professionals available to them. Rather, program heads believe their role is to direct advancement staff, charging them to come up with the brochures they want or the press releases they want or the students they want. They do not collaborate with advancement people in a professional way to develop a powerful, integrated strategic plan for accomplishing all these things and much more.

COMPETING FOR RESOURCES

Much of academic administrative life involves competing for scarce resources. Academic deans, although they appear to be close colleagues in some respects, often compete with each other for resources. So do vice presidents and everybody in advancement. Goals are set—in terms of enrollment, money, and visibility—but advancement professionals still have to compete for the resources required to meet them. Success in the race for resources requires political savvy and being in the right place at the right time. Sometimes just showing up is the most critical factor.

GET OUT OF YOUR BOX

Whether you are the boss or a frustrated practitioner, the first step to gain political savvy is finding a way out of your box. To do this you need to be seen around campus and contribute ideas outside your area of expertise. If you expect someone else to do this for you, you are, in fact, your own biggest problem.

A typical example is a communication staff member who tells the vice president he is extremely disappointed that he was not considered for an open director's job. The vice president is astonished. He never dreamed this person was interested in moving up. The staff member always did his job well, seemed perfectly content, and never demonstrated the slightest interest in moving up. He never ventured outside his "box," either physically or by the way he contributed in meetings or to other projects.

BUILDING RELATIONSHIPS AND COALITIONS

Knowing a lot of people is helpful, but building strategic relationships is professionally critical. Think about whom you need on your side, what it will take to get them there, and how to go about doing it.

Make three lists of internal opinion leaders:
- those who are generally positive about your interests
- those who are generally negative about your interests
- those who seem neutral

You may be tempted to go directly to the negatives and make every effort to change their minds. Big mistake. You will waste time trying to convert negative people, and with many you will fail. They are more likely to become even more adamant about their point of view. It is like trying to turn Republicans into Democrats. Try as you might, you will only make them better Republicans.

Do not waste time trying to change a person's mind, even if that person is a highly placed academic leader. These people may quietly come around when they see support for you building, or they may step out of the way. Better to reinforce your supporters and then, with the help of those supporters, focus on the neutrals. But you can solidify and broaden support only with constant attention, which requires out-of-the-box, face-to-face relationship building in meetings and one-on-ones.

MAKING DEALS

Distasteful as it may seem, making deals is actually good strategy, especially if do not have to compromise your beliefs or your programs. For example, you want to launch an advertising program and need the academic provost to help you get the money from the budget. In this case, find something the provost wants to do that you can help make happen. Then quietly suggest to the provost that this can be a win-win proposition. And it truly can. Of course, when this kind of deal-making is taken to extremes, other executives can get hurt. But that is not what we are talking about here. This is about starting win-win conversations that produce essential support and become opportunities to explain in more detail what you can do for the institution.

Sometimes it helps to visualize the organizational landscape in terms of wars and battles. Make a list of battles you might need to fight in order of importance to your overall program. You might have to be willing to lose a few battles to win the war. For example, you might withdraw a request when tension over the budget is running high in favor of doing something more important later. Timing in deal-making, as in most aspects of life, is everything.

USING THIRD PARTIES

This is an important tactic in all aspects of advancement work. Fund raisers use third parties to make "the ask." Third parties also place media stories, sell project ideas, and accrue internal political support for ideas and activities. Ask this question in everything you do: "Can I find someone else who would be more effective in this situation?"

Many advancement professionals do consulting for other professional organizations. Consultants from other campuses can often achieve results in a day or two that would take you months or years. This is an important lesson. The right consultant can be an effective third-party force for advancing new ideas.

HANDLING CONFLICT

Conflict resolution is another important tool. It involves thinking strategically instead of emotionally and requires objective analysis of the conflict followed by immediate and appropriate action.

The analytical process begins with getting to the roots of the matter. Is it a personality conflict? If so, you'll have to separate the people before the conflict can be resolved. Does someone think he or she has not been heard? If so, provide a serious forum and ask others really to listen this time. Then inform the person directly that he or she has been fully heard, and this is the decision. If the conflict is produced by a legitimate complaint, fix the problem.

But whenever conflicts arise, address them immediately—even if you think you cannot afford the time. Conflicts only get worse, and the time you lose by cutting them short will give you much more time later on. Also, unresolved conflicts will make everyone more hostile, the issue more divisive, and resolution much more costly than if you had addressed it at the beginning.

MOVING AHEAD

It is frustrating to reach a point in your career where you think you deserve a promotion but it just does not happen. A vice president once told a staff member in this situation, "There isn't anything wrong with you that a little success wouldn't fix, but I just don't have anything to offer right now."

If you really cannot be happy without a promotion, you have to leave. But weigh your values factors carefully. How important is a promotion? What are your options? Will this move set off a series of other moves, and are you prepared for that? How important is the money? How important is the city you live in? How much longer might it take to get a promotion where you are? If you stay long-term, will your salary increase enough over the years?

Clearly, professionals who move can climb from position to position more quickly; they often improve their salary more quickly as well. But for others, quality-of-life factors make the situation look different. These are all very personal and difficult decisions. But all of us must face them.

THE TRAP OF DOING A GOOD JOB

Another major professional frustration is to realize that doing a great job has become a problem for you. Your boss acts "funny" when someone else asks for your expertise, or you are denied access to certain people in a setting that obsessively follows proper channels. This situation is horrible for advancement professionals who need to work directly with many people. Bosses who fail to see that top-performing subordinates make them look better lack the self-confidence essential for effective leadership. This is another situation where, unless your coalition of supporters can facilitate a strategic rescue, you should consider moving on. Just as you need to gain support for your projects, having a coalition in place can save the day.

A PROPHET IN ONE'S OWN LAND

Many professionals who achieve prominence in their field face unanticipated problems at home. Suddenly, instead of being congratulated for their achievement and recognition, people on campus act as if they have become "too big for their britches." This happens to faculty members and staff alike. People start to ask where they find the time to pursue these "outside interests" and wonder if they are getting their job done at home. It may be simple envy, but it catches many by surprise when it happens.

Although many people in this difficult situation think about looking for another job, it is really a matter of learning how to cope with their new professional stature. Most people who achieve prominence learn how to keep their coalitions in place and live happily in a slightly different world.

GIVING CREDIT TO OTHERS

It is important to give credit to others—even when the credit should go to you. This does not mean your role should be invisible. But you should recognize the team for individual and collective achievements, and always take the time to recognize the achievements of colleagues. One of the more awful traits of administrative leaders is their inability to fully feel joy over the accomplishments of fellow administrators. Overcoming a tendency to under-praise colleagues goes a long way toward building your own long-term support base.

Nothing replaces preparation. Showing up fully prepared impresses everyone. At the same time that you schedule meetings, schedule earlier times to plan them. When you are asked to make a presentation, do it well. If a PowerPoint presentation is called for, prepare a good one. Earn the reputation that you never go anywhere unprepared.

THINK PROCESS

Leaders today must be organizational process-oriented. They must resist the temptation to say, "I do not have the time to listen." They must involve the right people in the discussion. They must realize that "buy-in" is essential to progress, and that buy-in happens only when people participate in the process. This especially applies to making difficult decisions. Most real professionals will go along with things they dislike as long as they received an honest hearing before the decision is made. Apply this principle to all you do.

Cultivate sincere interest in watching other talented people perform. Seeing people succeed at what you enabled them to do is one of the joys of professional life. Watching creativity happen can be exciting, and there is no limit to the potential of well-developed teams. They will shape the future of institutions in the years ahead.

THE POWER OF PERSISTENCE

Never, never, never give up. This may be the most important message of all. In institutions, every major stride forward seems to take forever. But persistence year after year is what makes it all work. When you think you are getting nowhere, look back over your shoulder. Almost always you will be able to say, "Wow, look how far we have come!"

Stay positive no matter what. Focusing on problems creates a negative environment. Focusing on what has worked stimulates good feelings. Knowing the risks is important, and making good decisions accordingly is critical. Determining which risks to take and which to avoid requires an advantages-disadvantages analysis. But maintaining an overriding positive context throughout the analysis is critical to long-term success. Never develop a pessimistic or sour attitude. If you feel one coming on, take a vacation. Or retire.

EXECUTIVE TRANSITIONS

After the president or your immediate boss leaves the institution, a difficult period of adjustment invariably follows. It is natural, it happens to everyone, and getting through it is part of professional life.

First, realize this is a time to determine what you want to do. Is there more for you to do here? Is it a good time to look elsewhere? After the new person arrives, while he or she evaluates your potential on the new team, evaluate how you feel about working with the new person. You may choose to make a change, but the decision to stay or go should be a mutual one.

The onset of a new leader can potentially renew the organization, always a positive development. The new leader will have to decide whether you are likely to help lead a future new day or if others will see you as too tied to the former administration. The big question: Can you get excited about orchestrating a completely new administrative era? If so, tell your new boss that is how you feel and that you would like to have enough time to demonstrate your commitment. During any transition, it is more secure to lead change than to resist change. If you honestly feel like resisting, it is probably time for you to go.

PERSONAL AND PROFESSIONAL DEVELOPMENT

Thorough management and leadership education will be critically important for both advancement and academic leaders of the future. How they get this education really does not matter, but they will have to have it.

Universities, as learning institutions, will have to do more to meet their own professional and leadership development needs. Understanding the political, organizational, and human dynamics of academic institutions will be instrumental to orchestrating their renewal. The world no longer will be patient. Never before has there been such urgent need for leaders who can embrace internal academic needs and cultures at the same time they deal with external economic and political realities. This is a complex challenge indeed, and we are going to have to face it head on.

CHAPTER 14

ORGANIZING ADVANCEMENT
TO MEET THE CHALLENGE

As advancement confronts intensified challenges, institutions strive to determine the best way to structure the related professions. Traditionally, advancement has consisted of three areas:

- development (or fund raising)
- communications (or institutional relations)
- alumni relations

This basic structure is known in the business as "the three-legged stool." But there has always been discussion about where government relations offices fit into all this. And once marketing emerged as a major force, similar discussions have addressed that.

Indeed, in some institutions the traditional model still works well. In others, however, the pressures of competition and social change raise questions about the proper place for the emerging area of advancement services as well as admissions and even athletics. Many institutions are in the process of determining the best organizational structure for dealing with the immediate pressures.

MARKETING EMERGES

Not too long ago, higher-education marketing as we know it today was virtually nonexistent. As recruiting students became more competitive and desire to refine institutional identities increased, institutions began to adapt basic marketing concepts to the academy. At first, communicators argued that this was nothing new. Marketing, they asserted, just used different terminology, that is, what marketing called "segments," communication called "audiences." And besides, marketing addressed only customers for its products, while communications addressed all publics.

When it became clear that marketing represented a new kind of institutional management thinking, questions about its positioning within the organization arose. Marketing asked all university managers to think about their products, how they delivered them, what they cost, and how to communicate information about them as a part of the overall planning process. Indeed, the marketing mentality applied to building relationships with important segments or markets, not only to people buying the products.

In some institutions marketing is separate from communications; in others, the word "marketing" as well its function are linked directly with communications. But most institutions embrace marketing, at least to some degree, and create structures that facilitate a marketing perspective. More will be doing so soon. The better marketing addresses vital issues, the higher its position in the organizational hierarchy.

ADMISSIONS ENTERS THE PICTURE

In most institutions, concern about enrollment is the primary impetus for bringing marketing into the picture. Schools that need more or better or different students view marketing as a way to improve the admissions process.

Prospective students and parents have become shoppers for education, no longer intimidated by the college selection process. School counselors and professional consultants help them shop around for the schools that best suit them and the best financial deals they can get. As the admissions marketplace changes, universities need to make greater use of basic marketing concepts.

The admissions process involves three types of personnel. The first are the people who recruit and counsel prospective students and parents. These people are often young; sometimes they are recent graduates of the university. They travel a lot, and they are trained first to recruit students and then counsel them through the admissions process. They are called professional counselors, but they are really the frontline sales force.

The second area consists of the people who process applications. These people maintain admissions standards and decide who is offered admission. They keep records and process the flow of information. They maintain the computer system that produces the data that will guide future recruiting and marketing strategies.

In the third area are personnel who do the strategic thinking related to brand-identity development, perform research on specific target markets, create related messaging and content, produce support publications and materials, handle admissions-related advertising, and manage the timing and flow of the communication process.

To avoid compromising academic standards, the first two areas are typically located within the admissions operation, where they report to the academic division of the university. To facilitate a smooth transition into campus life, some admissions operations report to the student affairs division. In rare cases, the marketing and communication area is attached to admissions, but it is more often located within advancement and provides services to admissions.

The pressures of competition, however, have made many institutions realize that the three areas of admissions function better when they work closely together. Many institutions have combined admissions with marketing and communication, and some have actually removed marketing and communication from its traditional place in the advancement division. Another reason for the split is that the fund-raising and alumni relations areas of advancement now face pressure-related issues of their own.

POSITIONING ADVANCEMENT FOR SUCCESS

The pressure to raise more money is forcing head fund raisers to eat and sleep raising money. They report directly to the president, work closely with the president on a daily basis, and devote little time to anything else. It remains appropriate for marketing and communication to be a part of advancement; but sometimes it is impossible for advancement vice presidents to lead broader divisions—especially when marketing and communication are expected to work closely with admissions and on overall reputation building. What's more, many new presidents are so obsessed with fund raising that they want both a fund-raising professional and a marketing professional to report directly to them and to function as a part of the executive leadership team.

ORGANIZATIONAL MODELS

Traditional. In the traditional model, the development director, alumni relations director, and communications director report directly to the vice president for advancement, who reports to the president. If there is a marketing director, he or she reports to the communications director. This model positions marketing to oversee research, handle advertising, and launch special events and projects.

Modified traditional. The organizational chart for this arrangement resembles the traditional model, as do formal reporting relationships. What's different is that the communications director also sits on the president's council. In some cases, the communication director's role is advisory, but in others it involves full participation. It is assumed that the communication director represents the marketing perspective as well. Depending on the personnel involved and their attitudes about reporting channels, this arrangement can work well but may become awkward. While the communications person participates at the cabinet level, his or her budget still comes through the advancement vice president.

Marketing split. It is increasingly common to create a separate marketing and communication division that reports directly to the president. Public relations, marketing, special events, and publications report to this new division, and the advancement vice president supervises only development and alumni relations. Some kind of liaison arrangement usually exists. For example, an advancement communications officer may work as a member of the marketing and communication team but be physically located in and serve only the development and alumni relations office.

PR/marketing/fund raising split. Less common are arrangements in which public relations, marketing, and fund raising all have their own senior officers. Under this arrangement, donor relations, alumni relations, government relations, internal relations, and media relations report to a senior public relations specialist. The marketing area might include admissions, advertising, program sponsorship development, etc. And, of course, the fund-raising people focus exclusively on fund raising.

Independent schools model. Independent schools are smaller and therefore have smaller executive teams. As they embrace marketing and respond to new fund-raising pressures, new positions and configurations emerge. The school superintendent and other unit heads may report to a headmaster, but public relations, alumni relations, donor relations, and marketing positions are often under the superintendent.

OTHER EMERGING AREAS

Advancement services. This area usually includes donor research, computer records, and donor recognition; it is normally part of the fund-raising and alumni relations area.

Special events. Special events has become a much more strategic area of activity. What you communicate in an invitation, to whom it is addressed, the overriding message of each event, following up with effective communication, using design to reinforce the brand in publications and at the event setting make special events a powerful marketing and communication tool. There are official institutional events, academic events with special strategic importance, alumni events, athletic events, and donor events. Each of these areas usually handles its own events. But as institutions better understand the potential power of special events, questions arise as to whether one professional group should handle all events and where to locate that group within the organization.

Marketing research. While universities are in the business of research, they typically do little market research on their own industry.

They collect data but perform little actual research. Competition again underlines the need to publicize and support research. Effective marketing requires information on levels of awareness and attitude, pricing, customer satisfaction, and more. Many institutions are establishing offices that oversee research work and map out trends. Should these offices be a separate unit, or should they be combined with advancement services and donor research? And under which vice president should they be placed? These are important questions to ponder.

Managing the Web. While the institution's Web site is important to everyone, it is usually unclear where the operation should be housed. Faculty and some staff see it primarily as a communication and research tool. Others see it as a marketing tool. Some want it to look more like a viewbook, especially the front pages, while others think it should look like and be a directory.

There are two primary aspects of Web-site management: technical development and support, and content and look. Some want to house the site in the computer area, where content and design people can work closely with marketing and communication people. Others want to house it in marketing and communication, with computer folks providing technical service. More and more institutions divide the functions between the two areas. This is a growing administrative area that needs to find a place of its own within the organizational structure, a place where Web-site administrators will have regular access to institutional leadership.

USING CREATIVE PROCESSES

Most advancement professionals agree that no matter how many related units are grouped in the same division, there are many others to embrace and work with closely. Clearly, the planning and implementation of all advancement-related activities need to become more integrated.

Regardless of how divisions are organized, organizational culture and management philosophy must ensure that units work together on developing both strategy and tactics. Many institutions form steering committees and task forces to handle this, assuming that structural changes will evolve over time.

Integrated task forces. These work best when they are chaired by the institution's most effective champion of "marketing as a way of thinking" and report directly to the president. The president must strongly convey that his or her office is behind this project and that he or she expects cooperation from task force members no matter what their formal reporting lines.

Such task forces will include the people responsible for marketing and communication activities, as well as representatives of admissions, public relations, advertising, student affairs, athletics, the bookstore, student government, faculty senate, staff senate, schools and colleges, alumni, fund raising, continuing education, etc. Twelve to 15 is usually a good number, and membership can change slightly from year to year, depending on priorities. Some task forces include members from the campus police, marketing faculty, board of trustees, and community leadership.

Task forces usually begin with a brand clarification assignment. Then they identify research that needs to be performed and later coordinate special marketing and communication initiatives. As these projects roll out, it should become clear whether a more efficient overall administrative structure is required. When task forces identify special initiatives, action teams composed of strategists, writers, and designers from different units can be assembled with the full support of the task force and the authority of the president's office to act.

These cross-unit processes establish a culture of support. They get people out of lonely boxes, using the best talent available to advance individual units as energetically as they advance the whole institution. The entire institution will learn to appreciate participatory processes and the power of focused teams.

DETERMINING FACTORS

Management style and culture. Some institutions have traditions of top-down management with formal channels of communication and reporting. Members of such organizations do not feel free to work together outside those lines and worry about what their immediate supervisors are thinking. Personnel trained in this system are uncomfortable with more freedom; they enjoy knowing what is expected of them and who performs their evaluations. When these people become supervisors, they want to control their units with little or no outside interference.

Because this type of organization has the most difficulty adopting integrated processes, it will have the most difficulty meeting the challenges of the future. However, when the president decides to open up and make a priority of mobilizing the troops, change can slowly occur. And it is happening in many institutions today.

Other institutions long have espoused a collegial and participatory management orientation. With good leadership and the right expertise, such organizations will prosper in this new world. But leadership will have to be wise, inspirational, and entrepreneurial.

And it will have to have the right expertise at the table. Indeed, when the wrong people participate in participatory processes, big mistakes are made.

Immediate critical issues. As pressing needs materialize, the need to organize a direct response intensifies. Here are some of the factors that drive change:

1. **Anticipated enrollment decline** motivates institutions to establish closer ties between the admissions department and the marketing and communication department.

2. **Need for visibility** motivates the institution to position marketing and communication so that it can spend more time developing brand identity and planning comprehensive visibility campaigns.

3. **Need for money** motivates the institution to remove units from advancement so that the head of advancement can concentrate on working directly with the president on a continuous, intensified fund-raising program.

4. **Need to revitalize the organization.** A variety of organizational changes are spurred by external and internal criticism that the institution has plateaued and needs to get moving again.

5. **Launching a new administration.** A change in structure can signal a new day for an institution. Positioning leaders in a new configuration lets new ideas and programs emerge.

Presidential preference. The kind of new leader described in this book is likely to have his or her own ideas about the necessary people and talent. They will form dynamic creative teams that reflect their priority values and the ideas related to the vision.

NO ONE MODEL

Although like others in many ways, every educational institution is unique. Each has different management styles, organizational cultures, and traditions. And all are at different stages of their own evolution and development. Some already are comfortable with "marketing" the institution, while others still think it means turning their institution into a shopping center. In some institutions, the faculty blames the administration for being slow to aggressively market the institution; in others, faculty still cringes at the very thought of marketing.

But this is changing fast. Reality is an effective change agent. Most professionals in all fields understand that the academy will have to change to survive, and that their very jobs may be at stake. After all, change can be good. And in time, it can revitalize us all.

CHAPTER 15

WHAT ABOUT ATHLETICS?

It is difficult for people outside the United States to understand how important athletic programs are to many universities here. The "sound mind in a sound body" concept always has been part of the full collegiate experience, but the extension of that fundamental idea into a businesslike operation with huge commitments and budgets often makes it seem like the tail wagging the dog.

Indeed, athletic programs create visibility and have other benefits that U.S. institutions can eloquently articulate. But as they look ahead to an intense competitive future, institutions will perform cost-benefit evaluations of their athletic programs. And they will reach different results depending on the number of students and alumni, the competition for the entertainment dollar in the local market, and the proportion of athletics expenditures in the overall budget. Changing conference affiliations and broadcast-income relationships will be factors as well.

Before examining the problems, consider the benefits that seem to be so important.

Name recognition. Name recognition is a significant factor in the success of any institution. Over the years, competing in sports, especially in popular sports such as football and basketball, has guaranteed widespread name recognition. The school's name appears in major newspapers before and after every game, in advertisements for the games, in ticket mailings and promotions, and in feature stories about the athletic program. All this combines to make an institution well known.

In the past, this kind of visibility would give institutions a reputation as a "football school" or a "party school" that would work against its academic standing. Today, though, the public does not make that kind of association. Rather, the public believes that if they have heard of your institution, it must be good.

Certainly, admissions counselors at unknown colleges are at a distinct disadvantage. They have to communicate so much before listeners feel familiar enough with the institution to want to know more. But when counselors from name-recognized colleges and universities begin to explain their institution's academic benefits, listeners feel they already know them.

Name recognition then is a shortcut to a good reputation, especially when it is accompanied by communications trumpeting the school's academic and cultural excellence. The value of visibility from athletics is determined by how much you need visibility to succeed as an academic institution and what the athletics program costs.

Vitality and school spirit. Americans have grown up around fall college football weekends and basketball games in winter and spring. Fewer, but still a significant number, enjoy other college sporting events. The contagious excitement of sports adds a pleasurable dimension to campus life. Rooting for your campus team fosters pride in and commitment to your institution, and it motivates alumni to stay involved over the years.

Many people who enjoyed college life want the fun to continue after graduation. As alumni they stay involved mostly by attending athletics events, and they establish a commitment to the institution accordingly. Athletic events become instrumental to fund raising, motivating alumni to give, especially as they get older and become more successful.

But the student body on some campuses has changed. Despite efforts to attract them, fewer and fewer attend games. At major state-supported universities, they may stay away because stadiums are filled with alumni and local people with season tickets. Or perhaps students are more interested in professional sports, especially big games shown on big screens at sports bars. Some students actually go to sports bars when their own college team is playing on campus.

The student athlete. Over the years, institutions have emphasized the value of intensely competitive athletics to student athletes. The discipline of training and hard work and the opportunities to develop leadership skills are experiences that translate directly to the world of work. The college experience is a huge factor in the real-world success stories of many former student athletes. The experience of winning and losing—and of coming back from losing to play again—gives athletes close-to-real-life experiences they never get in classrooms. Athletes learn invaluable lessons by meeting the challenge of studying, taking tests, and getting an education while training and practicing and competing. Certainly, intramural sports in no way offer similarly intense competitive experiences.

Of course, the opposing argument is that collegiate athletics has become an ultra-competitive environment that encourages athletes to have unrealistic dreams of becoming professionals. Athletes do not get a good education, and they suffer for it.

For some institutions, athletics has become a cost-benefit issue: How much does athletics cost in terms of the number of students who benefit? Of course, combine the benefits—widespread visibility, exciting school spirit and vitality, the student athlete experience—and many institutions conclude that their growing commitment to intercollegiate sports is justified. But how long can that continue? At what point does athletics just cost too much?

THE ISSUES AHEAD

Most organizations calculate cost-benefit to determine whether to maintain increasingly expensive endeavors. Some academic institutions calculate the partial benefit of athletic expenditures by computing the advertising value of the column inches of coverage their teams receive in newspapers nationwide. To that they add the value of any free public-service promotion they get and the time volunteers spend talking about the institution's athletics and academics to others. The total value, which can be quite high, can demonstrate positive cost-benefit to doubting critics.

Many academic institutions run athletics deficits; the few public institutions that sell out large stadiums are the exceptions. Some deficits are relatively small, while others are growing quite large. Institutions with "reasonable" deficits consider them a prudent marketing expense. The cost of buying that much visibility would be much greater. But depending on the institution's size, tolerance of deficits may be ending. The cost of competitive athletic programs today may have risen higher than the cost of buying the visibility. And some institutions argue that buying visibility would allow them to get visibility where it would be most productive.

Mounting costs. Travel to away games, escalating coaches' salaries, and increasing scholarship costs are only part of the problem. Other major expenses are costly facilities to attract the most talented athletes: weight-training centers, indoor practice fields, cutting-edge technology, and academic learning centers. These luxuries are driving up costs rapidly at a time when many institutions can't fill their stadiums. Costs are going up fast, and revenues are not keeping pace.

Maintaining the fan base. Broadcast income has become very important. But how much of it an institution gets depends on the terms of the athletic conference's contract with the networks and how many of its games are broadcast each season. Additional considerations are the size of the media market and the potential broadcast audience for games. Major state universities that perennially win in a locality where there are few other entertainment options fill their stadiums and receive ample broadcast revenue. But smaller schools in unfavorable locations that have up-and-down seasons are likely to struggle.

Today, broadcast networks have major impact on scheduling, and they schedule games at times when it can be difficult to fill stadiums. Football games may be scheduled on weeknights, basketball and other sports at all sorts of odd times. Games may be played at times when people would rather watch them on television or go to their child's soccer practice. The fallout is that people do not come to the stadium, ticket income diminishes, and the fan base fades as well. It is a real contradiction: You need additional broadcast revenue, but attaining it might cost you your fan base and, therefore, a large part of your fund-raising base.

Some schools perform market research to determine what will get people back to the games. Alumni and community people are surveyed. Students are surveyed. People known to spend money attending other sports are surveyed. What will attract them back to college games? What will attract families? What will get the students out of sports bars and into the stadium? And at many institutions, what will get people away from tailgate parties in the stadium parking lot and into the stadium to watch the game?

Marketing people are taking many initiatives. They produce mailings and advertising more targeted to special interests. They intensify promotional activities, with particular emphasis on year-round ticket sales. They take heroic initiatives to attract people to the stadium: pre-game carnivals for families, parking lot entertainment for tailgaters, pre-game ceremonies featuring celebrities and novelties, military flyovers, half-time extravaganzas, fireworks and sound effects throughout the game, giveaways, and discounts.

WHERE WILL IT END?

In this changing environment, many institutions are trying to figure it all out. Successful programs look for better deals, which often lead to conference realignments, another costly situation for many schools. Schools have to buy their way into conferences—and buy their way out. That's expensive, as is redoing travel budgets and everything else associated with each move. And with each conference change, the broadcast contract changes too. Presumably, the changes will be for the better, but it does not always stay that way for long. New contracts eventually end and have to be renegotiated, and the situation often gets even more complicated.

Most programs, even smaller ones, are too deeply committed to athletics to pull the plug abruptly. And, besides, the unintended consequences can be enormous. Indeed, costs can be cut, but by how much? Should schools eliminate athletics programs altogether or just downscale? When they scale down, many institutions find that smaller programs in smaller conferences still are costly, and that public interest and revenues drop sharply, too. The financial problems are not solved. Moreover, many institutions cannot imagine having no athletics program at all.

Most institutions will ride this horse much farther because, while they see no other solution now, they believe they will find one eventually. Their alumni bodies cannot imagine the school without athletics, and major donors still are connected largely through their love of the college athletic experience. If stadium audiences are dwindling because current students are losing enthusiasm and families do not attend anymore, and the games are becoming fringe-time cable television shows, the economic realities might prompt schools with similar problems to get together to find a way to make it all make sense.

WHAT MIGHT LIE AHEAD

In the United States, intercollegiate athletics is likely to remain part of the college experience long into the future. It will continue to be a marketing tool that creates visibility, a source of campus vitality, and an object of love of many alumni. But economic realities will bring about changes and even more conference volatility.

While sports give American institutions national and international exposure, institutions obtain most of their enrollment and support from within their region. This is likely to continue because, while students are becoming more globally oriented in some ways, most still want to go to colleges close to home. Families want to visit students more often, and students want to feel away from home but still connected. Consequently, regional athletic programs that establish regional visibility make more marketing sense.

Indeed, the desire for national visibility is usually more a matter of vanity than a marketing necessity. The student market and donor base should view the institution as nationally and internationally significant because of what faculty do, where students travel to study, what academic work is stressed, and how and to whom this is communicated. What's critical is that you are visible to those who control your future well-being and that *they* believe you are nationally and internationally significant. Strategically, most of the people you have to reach are located in your region. Consequently, athletics expenditures will continue to be seen as a marketing expense.

Smaller conferences. While the huge, successful programs will continue to flourish for a very long time, thinking regionally is likely to produce smaller, more regional conferences that reduce travel distances, make cable broadcasts more regional, and establish intense rivalries. Similar institutions will compete with each other on a playing field that is more level, both financially and programmatically.

Smaller stadiums. Smaller stadiums that are easier to fill are likely to materialize. Alumni, students, and community people will feel more excited about the collegiate stadium experience and generate more word-of-mouth exuberance. In some communities, smaller-scale competition might come to resemble minor-league baseball clubs, where all the things colleges are doing now to attract families will work better for them. Operations will be scaled down, but the community and family spirit that evokes loyalty will grow.

Fewer athletic scholarships. Smaller regional programs will put less emphasis on recruiting the very top athletes. Institutions will appraise the prospects of post-college professional careers realistically and authentically portray what the total college experience is likely to mean in the future. They still will offer scholarships, but fewer of them, which will make budgets more manageable too.

Appropriate salaries. Talented staff should earn good salaries—in both academics and athletics. But there is a difference between good salaries and a system out of control. After all, university careers offer a lifestyle benefit to all academics, staff members, and coaches.

WHAT WILL REALLY HAPPEN?

Changes in institutions are driven by economics and organizational momentum. Changes in athletics will be gradual, introduced over time as constituency pressures change and economic necessities appear. I have mentioned a few possibilities, but change always brings surprises.

For example, a university's constituencies are likely to become more regional in one way and more global in another. Their attitudes and interests are likely to change in ways difficult to predict. More U.S. universities will establish campuses abroad, probably closer to Asia. Foreign students are likely to enroll at those overseas campuses but spend time at the U.S. campuses. And while U.S. students will do a good portion of their studies at foreign locations, they will enroll at campuses closer to home. How will the global migration of students affect local campus communities? How will this affect traditional college athletics? Obviously, no one knows for sure, but it is certain change will come—and it might be sooner rather than later.

CHAPTER 16

TEACHING INSTITUTIONS
A NEW WAY OF THINKING

To maintain their independent, free-spirited role in this rapidly changing world, institutions have to learn a new way to think about moving forward. Although teachers and scholars generally know better than prospective students what students need to know, to remain competitive, institutions will have to meet students where they are—and do it while maintaining academic integrity.

At first, this may seem contradictory. Many academics see marketing as a process that finds out what people want and then gives it to them. They cannot handle that thought, and indeed they should not. But this is not true about all kinds of marketing, and it is not true about higher-education marketing. Marketing in higher education means determining students' perceived needs and connecting with them. It also means leading students on an exciting search for personal meaning and career success that can be discovered only along the way in the educational adventure.

A LEARNING ORGANIZATION

By definition universities are learning organizations. They exist to discover and report new knowledge, produce creative objects and ideas, and design learning opportunities for individuals. But dedication to learning does not always translate into providing managers and leaders with the professional development they need to stay on top of changes in the higher-education industry, to make plans, and to lead organizations.

To create a learning organization, executive management must keep up with the latest ideas in education and leadership, and it must offer an ongoing program of learning opportunities for every opinion leader and unit leader in the institution. The institution has to be learning and changing itself along with its students.

DEVELOPING A MARKETING PERSPECTIVE

As explained previously, marketing is a way to simultaneously think about and plan the programs you offer, the way you present them, how you price them, and how you communicate them. Marketing provides a context for all other business and management functions. Its major contribution is constantly to remind constituents that everything the organization plans must take into account external economic, social, and educational trends. Organizations cannot be planned only from the inside. They cannot just make up where they want to go or what they do best. They must take into account the historical realities of what they have done well, why they have done well, and the characteristics of the marketplace that have been their lifeblood. Organizations can alter direction, revitalize, and even change course, but they cannot abruptly turn into something they have never been.

Traveling to campuses around the world has taught me that one of the biggest mistakes academic institutions make is to believe that they can compete instantly with aspirant institutions that are not their actual competitors. The danger of benchmarking these competitors is that it makes you think studying them enables you to quickly emulate and thereby compete successfully with them. This strategy will never work because usually there are strong reasons why your competitors are who they are. By imitating aspirant institutions, you could lose your foundation market and find yourself perennially behind an institution that resembles you in some ways but has a different historical market base. Exceptions to this are rare.

Institutions need to understand their historical roots, natural foundation marketplace, and what they do well—and then chart a future based on becoming the world's best at doing just that. Taking all these factors into account, each institution is truly unique. Before everyone responsible for moving the place ahead can agree on these factors, structured learning must take place. It is a matter of becoming marketplace-sensitive without compromising the basic mission of the institution, or of higher education.

Several education or training tools can be used to establish widespread understanding among opinion and unit leaders and, as a result, establish a common foundation for effective strategic planning.

TOOLS FOR ESTABLISHING A LEARNING ORGANIZATION

Briefings for unit and opinion leaders. Introduce this new way of thinking at 90-minute sessions with unit and opinion leaders. If a respected internal champion of the process exists, ask this person to facilitate. Otherwise, use an outside consultant. The subject matter is simple. It includes:

1. The basics of integrated marketing, as a way of thinking and as a way of bringing people in different units together.

2. How to set up integrated processes, from task forces to editorial priority committees to action teams.

3. The basics of segmentation and how it facilitates direct and inter-active communication.

4. How integrated communication differs from promotion, its basis on the realities of a changing news business and the power of one-to-one relationship building.

5. Why differentiating the institution is the most basic step in establishing competitive advantage and how to go about it.

6. Why the institution itself is the fundamental "product" the student buys and the reason why developing the "brand" is so important. Also, how to see and communicate specific schools, colleges, and programs as "sub-brands" in a larger context.

7. How to understand the basic marketing concept of "distribution," both in the context of teaching and learning and in the context of campus lifestyle-based services.

8. How to examine the many dimensions of "quality." Quality in higher education usually was equated to "selectivity," but today's education consumer defines it more in terms of access to faculty, class size, how services are delivered, staff and faculty attitudes about service, help in finding jobs, etc.

9. Elements of an effective marketing plan, or blueprint, emphasizing that the format should be simple and easily communicated, the process should be ongoing, the plan should focus on a few special initiatives that can make the most difference, and

eventually the marketing plan should merge with the strategic plan. As established earlier, if the strategic plan has an overall marketing orientation, or vice versa, one plan will suffice and be easiest for everyone to understand and implement.

10. Emphasis on the role of leadership. Everyone must come to understand the various dimensions and challenges of real leadership and why it is critical to moving institutions forward. Competitive advantage can be defined, special initiatives identified, and effective marketing materials produced. But unless everyone walks the talk, the organization simply will not move ahead.

Another approach is to present something like "10 steps to an integrated marketing program." Instead of introducing the basic subject matter and letting people infer what to do, this approach communicates the steps to take.

Start by stating the objective: To adapt the latest thinking on integrated and relationship marketing to the academy to enhance competitiveness and organizational effectiveness, especially as they relate to visibility, admissions, fund raising, alumni relations, curriculum planning, student program planning, and morale.

The rest of the briefing presents and discusses the 10 steps:

1. Set up an internal education process to establish marketing as a way of thinking throughout the organization, concentrating on opinion leaders.
2. Clarify mission and vision, translate them to a message based on competitive advantage, and then get everyone on the same page.
3. Establish a strategic marketing task force as an activity of the CEO's office, and find a champion to manage it.

4. Identify marketing segments and opinion leaders within those segments, including internal ones.
5. Perform an audit of current marketing and communication operations and materials to determine consistency of identity, message, and intensity and assess readiness to implement a fully integrated program.
6. Establish ongoing survey and focus-group research for each market segment to assess awareness, attitude, knowledge, and pricing elasticity.
7. Determine priorities and set goals, such as visibility with and more applications from specific segments.
8. Establish action teams for market-segment initiatives and then outline an action blueprint.
9. Focus on branding the institution and increasing visibility, clearly determining whom you want to reach and what it will cost.
10. Build feedback mechanisms into the total process as a part of research, planning discussions, and all communications.

Use opinion leader and unit-head briefings to establish a widespread, common understanding of what integrated marketing is all about. An ensuing operations audit will reinforce many of the same concepts, while gathering information about the organization's capacity to implement an integrated process.

EDUCATIONAL ROLE OF AUDITS

In Chapter 4, I explained the operations audit process in some detail. I posited more than 25 topics as the basis for assessing consistency of message and perceived effectiveness of operations among advancement staff, as well as opinion and unit leaders all over campus. When performed properly, operations audits collect information and communicate the basics of integrated marketing.

Assuming that audit participants have attended a briefing beforehand, the audit should reinforce the basic subject matter and offer opportunities for one-on-one encounters and small-group discussions on how marketing and communication has worked in the past and how it can maximize impact in the future.

When the audit is complete and compiled into a report, assemble those who attended briefings and participants in the audit to hear an executive summary version. This is yet another opportunity to review the basics of the subject and discuss the importance of a clear identity and strategic planning.

Once integrated marketing becomes part of the institutional vocabulary, establish a modified updating process to keep the conversation and evaluation process alive. Reporting the results of these updates provides ongoing opportunities for leadership to gather and discuss progress and continuing challenges.

CLARIFYING IDENTITY

I have already explained how to operate identity-clarifying workshops and who should attend them (see Chapter 6). But it is important to note the role of these workshops in the total education process. Identity-clarifying workshops are completely interactive, small-group meetings that should follow opinion-leader and unit-head briefings.

In a nutshell, selected leaders gather to work through a series of questions designed to clarify and unify thinking related to the institution's brand. The ensuing discussion elicits questions and stimulates conversations that enhance understanding of, and commitment to, the entire program. Thus the meeting serves a very important educational role as well.

REENERGIZING THE ADVANCEMENT STAFF

The subject matter of integrated marketing is no longer new to professionals in every part of advancement. But using integrated marketing to influence what fund-raising and alumni relations people plan and do might be quite new. Even if it is not, make sure all practitioners understand the terms and processes in the same way. These people must share a complete understanding of the subject matter and its benefits and be honestly committed to making it work.

Rethinking the basics together is the best way to bring about a shared understanding, an aspect of the educational process that requires creation of a "professional development master class." Taught by a top expert in the field, the class should let advancement and other marketing professionals question the teacher and adapt the material to their own operations. The class should show how to put these principles to work realistically in each area, within each staff group, and within each budget.

Here is a way to organize a master class that could be called "Marketing the Academy in the 21st Century":

Part I. A way of thinking:
1. Understanding the changing market
2. International issues and trends
3. Adapting integrated marketing to the academy
4. Dealing with the changing news business
5. Affordable research and how to do it

6. Building our brand
7. When to advertise and what kind to do
8. Auditing the operation on an ongoing basis
9. Designing an effective action plan, or blueprint

Part II. Implementation:
1. Tested processes and strategies
2. Internal marketing tactics
3. Impact on student recruiting
4. Impact on alumni relations
5. Impact on fund raising
6. Impact on athletics
7. Rethinking community relations
8. Impact on overall strategic planning
9. Developing appropriate leadership at all levels
(For a complete outline of master class content, see Appendix D.)

Adapt classes to suit the knowledge level of each staff member. But to develop a new or renewed common language and shared understanding of exactly what you realistically can accomplish in all areas of advancement, revisit the basics together. Let everyone see how this thinking applies to all of advancement, and how it can expand thinking about ways fund raising and alumni relations can meet the expectations of a changing and challenging world.

GETTING FOCUSED ON SPECIAL INITIATIVES
A byproduct of this educational process is an opportunity to refute the clichéd concern that all plans end up sitting on a shelf somewhere.

Indeed, this is often the case with traditional planning processes, especially when the plan is too detailed and contains page after page of goals and objectives accompanied by page after page of supporting details. As stated earlier, the most effective plans are simple, easy to remember, and focused on the actions that will make the biggest difference.

The entire educational process is designed to introduce, develop, and reinforce identical ideas about integrated marketing. With all managers and leaders participating on an ongoing basis, the process orchestrates and mobilizes the total organization to implement a set of simple, focused initiatives that differentiate the organization and establish competitive advantage in a very complex and changing world.

CHAPTER 17

FINAL THOUGHTS

This book is based on direct observation, countless interviews and conversations, operations and materials assessments, interactive workshops, and executive seminars at campuses and conferences from the United States to Australia. As said in different ways and several times, our industry is going through a sea change that will present new and difficult challenges to the advancement professions. These challenges will bring new opportunities and give us a more central role in the academy, which is the good news. But new prominence will be accompanied by higher expectations, greater accountability, and the necessity to practice our crafts with greater sophistication.

I have argued that marketing is really a way of thinking, and that integrated marketing is a way to orchestrate total institutional awareness. I have said that marketing, now part of everyone's job, has gone from playing virtually no role in academic institutions to influencing change in every area of advancement, as well as in overall institutional strategic planning.

How do advancement professionals plan to handle this new responsibility? The elements of the learning institution (see Chapter

16) represent tangible initiatives. But here are some general suggestions for individual practitioners.

Keep the core questions in mind:
1. What core message (brand) will advance our institution?
2. How can we get everyone on the same page (planning process) with respect to that message?
3. What are the reputation-defining stories (editorial process) that will advance the core message and reinforce the defining culture?
4. What are the priority audiences (target markets)?
5. What do we need to know about these audiences (research) to connect with them?
6. What are the best ways (media tactics) to communicate with them?

While these are all key marketing questions, in a dramatically changing international marketplace, they become core institutional questions as well. As such, they are key framing questions for all advancement planning.

ELEMENTS OF SUCCESS

The right product(s). It is crucial to understand that institutions provide lifetime identities for students; this identity is the main product prospective students "buy." "Build it and they will come" no longer works. An institution must establish a powerful, appealing presence in the minds of the right people. Selecting programs that build and support that identity is the critical task of planning.

A strong identity. Your basic objective is to establish a competitive advantage in specific market targets. This requires strong differentiation, real emotional attraction, and consensus on what makes the institution special.

Sophisticated marketing. This simply means seeing the world as market segments, thinking strategically about ways to connect with them, appreciating the power of imaginative writing and creative design, realizing that special events are optimal communication opportunities, understanding that the news media are changing and are no longer reliable, and knowing that effective out-front leadership is the make-or-break factor.

The sad truth is that few institutions have enough talented people who think and act this way. And when these talented people are present, they are often taken for granted or rejected because they threaten traditional ways of thinking. Instead of rewarding and celebrating what works, too many people in too many institutions focus on the failures and on what they personally dislike. They create a negative, sour atmosphere in which to conduct a business that simply has to be positive, upbeat, and forward-thinking.

Spotting trends, seizing opportunities, and orchestrating forward-leaning, ongoing dynamics establish momentum, and this is what marketing and communication do. But there has to be substance. There must be a solid, high-quality steak producing the great-sounding sizzle. Starting and maintaining momentum through thick and thin is what an integrated approach does.

IT ALL STARTS INSIDE

Yes, marketing makes people think the process must start externally and build inside. You begin with an understanding of what the market needs and will respond to and then develop programs that meet those needs. Institutions often neglect that critical part of the formula.

But just as critical is the inside part of the formula. Academic institutions have founding missions, long-standing traditions, cultural entities, and program strengths that have evolved over time. You must have a deep understanding of those defining realities and find ways to match them with external market demands.

Getting everyone, or mostly everyone, on the same page is absolutely necessary for success. Time spent clarifying mission, vision, and values internally is time well spent. Make certain new faculty and staff orientation programs convey the central messages and brand characteristics. Edit internal publications with an eye toward building the culture. Train front-line people to walk the talk. And, of course, having everyone spread the word (once they know it) establishes the dynamic that all other materials and communications must effectively support.

EMBRACE OUR INTERNATIONAL STANCE
Worldwide government cutbacks have spurred new thinking about both fund raising and student recruiting. New thinking about pricing and where to find the best student markets of the future may quickly follow.

Other factors driving change include the economic emergence of Asia and U.S. hurdles to the admission of foreign students. Having noticed these changes, universities worldwide are upgrading their quality and rethinking their potential to attract students from everywhere and raise money from anywhere.

LEARN FROM EACH OTHER

Gone are the days when there was one right way to do things. There is no longer one right way to run a campaign, one right way to run a communications office, or one right way to organize an alumni program. And no longer does knowledge of every aspect of advancement reside exclusively in the United States. Many exciting programs are emerging around the world, and international meetings have become forums for a true exchange of ideas.

Professionals always have learned from each other; that is the purpose of professional meetings and conferences. Now there are compelling reasons to schedule and attend international meetings and conferences. While advancement professions have a longer history in the United States than in the rest of the world, institutions in many countries are making up for lost time. Sophisticated advancement programs now exist in Canada, the United Kingdom, Australia, and elsewhere. Indeed, they are coming on strong everywhere.

Peter Slee, deputy vice chancellor (student and staff affairs) of Northumbria University in England and chairman of the CASE Europe Board of Trustees, has led a consortium of U.K. universities engaged in a project to define marketing excellence in academic institutions. First, the consortium recognized that because the culture of each organization is different, there will be differences in the way marketing is organized and delivered. Because the core processes of marketing are the same everywhere, however, strategy and tactics can be standardized. And the collective need to deliver and assess "effectiveness" is a problem all share. The collaborative project thus has identified subject areas in which professionals worldwide can help one another.

Second, the consortium suggested that all marketing plans should be built around what they call "the student journey." Although this sounds obvious, few academic institutions anywhere actually do it. Focusing on the student journey means that marketing is a lifetime interaction with students. Institutions must know what students think they need before they enroll, through every stage of student life, and on into adulthood. This kind of sound thinking applies to other areas of advancement as well.

STUDY OTHER CULTURES, IDEAS

Because so much of the world's business is conducted in English, English-language degree programs in the Middle East, Asia, and other parts of the world have become prevalent.

But while English may be spoken in official circles, the most significant transactions occur in the local language. Indeed, everything of substance grows out of the area's culture, values, and ideas. Consequently, working internationally means becoming better informed about other cultures and the beliefs that drive attitudes and actions. Americans have been especially provincial about international involvement and oblivious of their need for these tools of academic commerce. But these tools will become critical to success in the years ahead.

BECOME MORE COMPETITIVE

In the United States, becoming more competitive can mean being overly aggressive, winning at all costs, making rivals into losers. But this is not necessary in the academic world. There is room for all kinds of institutions, and the greater the variety the better for consumers. They will have more high-quality options to choose from, and that will be a good thing.

Becoming more competitive means planning, managing, and communicating in ways that make institutions better known for what they do well. It means that institutions should think about how they are "positioned" in the growing international marketplace, and this thinking should be an ongoing preoccupation for institutional leaders at all levels.

BENCHMARKING CAN MISLEAD

The best benchmarking reveals what other institutions are doing and how they are doing it. This information is essential for your own planning, and it should be done with great care. "Best practices" further indicate factors that produce successful programs. But using that information to rationalize that "they have this amount of budget and this number of staff" can condemn you to never being better than number 2.

Whenever you model yourself after another organization, you almost always will play second fiddle. That may be acceptable for survival, but it is not a pathway to distinction. I have seen institutions, and sometimes the schools and colleges within them, obsess over modeling their competition. And to justify requests for support, I have seen top administrators ask deans and department heads to find out what the other place is doing. But when this information prompts duplication, the school or program has installed built-in limitations to success.

In *Good to Great*, Jim Collins describes how organizations rise from good to great. An organization that models a successful organization can be good, but only the ones that establish and build on their unique distinctions can become great. The great ones can proclaim with confidence that they are the best in the world at what they do.

The most serious criticism of university ratings by magazines is that when institutions use the magazine's standards to make planning decisions, they all become alike. Distinguished institutions capitalize on the characteristics that make them unique.

DEVELOP CREATIVITY

Creativity is an important topic in management and strategic planning these days. The challenge is to stay true to your roots, repeating messages and designs enough to make your identity visible while finding different and more compelling ways to do it. The power of design asserts itself in competitive situations.

Involving creative designers and writers in the earliest stages of planning can have a rewarding payoff. The core ideas they absorb at the beginning will be reflected accurately later. Also, many designers learn how to contribute creative content ideas by imagining their designs in advance. An entire issue of *Fast Company* magazine (June 2005), devoted to the power of design, details the major role of product designers, architects, and others in early strategic planning and priority setting. Creative writers contribute to the process too. In the future, higher education will have to have other types of organizations teach them how to differentiate themselves with creativity.

WORK IN TEAMS

Process takes considerable time. Deadline pressure forces people to get it done, which generally means assigning the best person to do it.

But setting priorities is a participatory process, and forming creative teams to implement those priorities is the best way to move an organization forward. It is motivational, and talented people working together inevitably generate better solutions than even the most talented individuals working alone.

Over time, creative teams generate the word-of-mouth effect necessary for excellent internal communication. Teams generally adhere to the spirit of participatory planning, clearly demonstrating that more people from more places can more effectively move the enterprise ahead.

STAY POSITIVE ALL THE TIME

Academics are problem-oriented. Most academic work involves figuring out what's wrong and then finding solutions. In fact, some strategic planning models are problem-oriented. They employ investigators to brainstorm problems and then perform an "advantages-disadvantages" analysis to find the best solutions.

But as discussed previously, a problem orientation can produce a negative climate, which is not at all inspiring. Better to identify what can make the place the "best in the world," figure out how to achieve it, and then create enthusiasm for forward movement with positive, inspiring talk. The best leaders are inspirational champions, not people who dwell on fixing what's wrong. And the best leaders are what higher education will need.

WORK HARD, PLAY HARD

Effective leadership really is a 24/7 preoccupation. Telling your best people to take more time off does not always work the way you expect. Many people cannot completely get away. Moving organizations ahead becomes an integrated experience for individuals, too, but they must learn how to work hard and play hard in short spurts.

Old-style managers generally avoided socializing with their employees. Creativity and inspiration, however, require a different approach. Most effective leaders can concentrate on work for periods of time and then let their hair down and have fun—sometimes with family and friends and at other times with their employees. Getting together socially, either at work or elsewhere, can be motivational. Employees can see their fellow professionals as real people and learn about their aspirations and pleasures. These are also moments when a word or two of important business might get exchanged in a more personal context.

Working hard and playing hard with colleagues can be a positive force in an integrated organization. It is good for fellow professionals to see that side of you. You become a real human being, and they will appreciate knowing you that way. "Getting away," therefore, becomes integrated with work, a practical solution for driven people. And it works better for the organization that intends to become better.

EVOLVE, NOT TRANSFORM

The best organizations stay grounded in their founding mission because that is what best differentiates them. Institutions were almost always founded by someone who saw a need that was not being met. "First" always bestows marketing advantage.

But staying grounded does not mean standing still. Rather, it means institutions must gradually adapt to the realities of a changing society. That is the strategic challenge: to change while remaining the same. What sounds like a paradox must become the institution's creative challenge. Some themes stay the same, while others must reflect the times.

REMEMBER VALUES, MISSION

Some leaders try to make over their institutions according to their personal vision of what an academic institution should be. These leaders ignore the institution's founding mission and long-established culture and values. This style of change-agent, even when highly placed in the organization, rarely succeeds. Too many people know deep inside that someone is trying to transform the place into something it is not, and they quietly resist. Eventually, the institution's cultural values and mission prevail.

Organizations are like organisms, the personnel its lifeblood. Organizations require careful treatment when they get sick or are injured, and some illnesses are more serious than others. But because organizations have minds of their own, the treatment affects the entire body. A good deal of care and patience may be required. But to neglect the illness, or the external forces that produced it, is certainly unwise and can be deadly.

Institutions stand firm only when they stand on solid values. It is the "how" that justifies continuation of the "what." Regardless of your personal feelings about medicine, holistic treatments must be practiced on organizations.

The most effective leaders are born to achieve, born to lead, and born to teach. Yes, born to teach. Teaching is an art mastered by all effective leaders, their creative outlet. The best leaders spend a great deal of time learning, and they constantly are looking for ways to pass on their learning to others—sometimes to staff and sometimes to anyone who will listen.

There is always debate about whether it is better to give the public what it wants or offer them what you have—and this debate should never end. Staying true to your foundational strengths while connecting with changing social needs always will be your challenge. In this regard, the need to know who you are while you adapt to a changing world is still another way institutions and individuals are very much alike.

MARKET-DRIVEN PARTICIPATORY STRATEGIC PLANNING GUIDE

Many strategic planning projects have most of the elements of a marketing plan. They address program objectives, facilities objectives, finance issues, pricing parameters, and more. A strategic plan begins with an environmental scan that identifies demographic trends, job trends, enrollment trends, growth trends, and all the indicators that explain how the marketplace is changing. If it also addresses the implications for effective marketing and communicating, the strategic plan becomes a marketing plan as well. In fact, if the two first and last components either are excluded from the strategic planning process or shortchanged in any way, the strategic plan could become irrelevant to the changing world.

If the strategic plan contains marketing and communication components, it must add a slightly more specific marketing and communication action plan that shows which special initiatives will advance the mission and the goals outlined in the strategic/marketing plan. Appendix B presents an outline for this kind of mission-driven, integrated marketing plan.

FIRST STEP: PRELIMINARY PLANNING ACTIVITIES

1. **Clarify the mission statement.** Some staff will want to rewrite the mission statement; appoint a committee to oversee this. Ask each major unit to organize groups to provide ideas to the committee. One option is to ask these groups to submit four or five phrases that express their understanding of the founding mission. The central committee then prepares a one- or two-sentence mission statement that captures the essence of the phrases submitted by the others.

Other institutions appoint a central committee to compose one- or two-sentence versions of their already lengthy official mission statements that can be approved by the executive cabinet and/or board for use in guiding, planning, and marketing.

It is important to clarify the mission prior to launching a participatory planning project. If it is not done, all groups and committees will determine they need such a statement and spend all their time developing one.

2. **Conduct an environmental scan.** As described above, it is critical to have information on the table about anticipated social change so that planning can decide how the institution can maintain its mission while staying relevant to the marketplace.

3. **Define parameters, restraints, and expectations.** Explain in advance any known parameters. For example, some institutions provide explanations of their endowment spending policies to preempt irrelevant talk about "taking money from savings." Information on related pricing elasticity studies also makes discussions more realistic.

In addition, tell participants up front that although they will come up with many more ideas than can be implemented, the institution does pledge to implement a good number of them. This is important because many participants will be skeptical, suspecting that this whole thing will turn out to be a waste of their time—especially when brainstorming begins to sound like compiling a wish list.

SECOND STEP: APPOINT A FUTURE PLANNING COMMISSION

One effective approach is to appoint a commission in which half of the participants come from inside the institution, and half come from outside. Appoint a high-profile volunteer chairmen as well as a project director selected from the executive staff.

Put task forces to work in areas such as the undergraduate experience, the role of graduate education, technology, community connections, alumni relations, the role of athletics, overall institutional positioning, and whatever seems relevant to your organization. Select an outside volunteer chair to work with an internal task-force facilitator. Ask each group to work over a specified period of time, for example, one year. Have them schedule their own meetings and determine whether to form subgroups. Charge them to present a list of suggestions, possibly 10 or so in priority order, to be included in a commission report. Again, point out at the project kickoff event that not all suggestions can be implemented, but promise to carry out a significant number of them.

Form additional task forces with volunteer chairs and staff facilitators for each school and college. Have them first perform a simple SWOT (strengths, weaknesses, opportunities, threats) analysis and then offer prioritized suggestions for enhancing programs.

THIRD STEP: COMMISSION REPORT

Stage a closing event to combine task force suggestions and publish a report. Tell all participants how important they have been and will continue to be in the future. For that reason, you will put them on a mailing list to receive updates and insider information about initiatives and accomplishments. The institution now has assembled the most important list it will ever have: opinion leaders able to control the organization's future health who will maintain ongoing, interactive, bond-building relationships with the institution.

FOURTH STEP: ACTION PLAN

A group of administrative leaders, possibly the cabinet or a larger group formed by the president, will take the suggestions and determine which to implement, in what order, and at what cost. Some will be "catch-up" projects, such as modernizing laboratories and classrooms, and others will be new initiatives that will give the institution additional distinctiveness.

This proposed action plan now can go to the trustees, along with recommendations on how to pay for the projects. Some projects can be funded by reallocating funds, while others can become goals for philanthropy. In this way, participatory planning commissions will serve as staging mechanisms for campaigns and the primary tools for developing the case for support.

Because the project began with a thorough environmental scan and one of the task forces addressed positioning and other marketing challenges, the final report can provide the primary substance of a marketing plan. Now you must create a marketing action outline, or blueprint (as explained in Appendix B), to connect recommended initiatives to mission and university goals.

MISSION-DRIVEN
MARKETING PLANNING GUIDE

With a marketing-oriented strategic plan in hand, you can outline a blueprint. Three types of groups can be used to develop a blueprint:

1. **Marketing task force.** This group consists of all key people involved in marketing all key areas. They are responsible for clarifying overall institutional brand identity, dealing with issues related to building brand identity as it relates to individual program sub-brands, and keeping one another informed about what they are doing.

2. **Marketing and communication executive committee.** This group generally consists of unit heads of the various communication areas. They are responsible for overseeing necessary research and overall implementation.

3. **Action teams.** Formed for each major marketing initiative, action teams consist of expert planners, researchers, writers, designers, promoters, and whoever else is needed to do the job with maximum talent and creativity. Members come from the task force, the executive committee, or anywhere else the best talent resides.

Eight-step action plan or blueprint outline:

1. **State the mission, vision, and values.** Prepare a shortened version—one or two sentences—if the official statement is too lengthy.

2. **Institutional goals.** If there are too many goals (more than five or six), combine and restate them. If you do, obtain approval of the president.

3. **Brand guidelines.** Outline the guidelines on one page (as discussed previously). Include a positioning statement of competitive advantage, a list of defining features/ benefits, facts that verify the existence of features/benefits, and the design elements that will represent the brand.
4. **Marketing goals.** State them as extensions of the (above) university goals.
5. **Priority market segments.** Identify groups that will be the focus of intense interactive marketing and communication.
6. **Research summary.** Include only the research findings that specifically inform marketing decisions.
7. **Marketing and communication goals for each segment.** Note what attitude, knowledge, or behavior is expected.
8. **Primary marketing initiatives for each segment.** These are the basic initiatives that, if carried out energetically, will achieve the marketing goals, advance the university goals, and generate the perception of stepping out.

CASE STUDY:
UNIVERSITY OF NEW BRUNSWICK, CANADA

Many institutions are in the process of implementing integrated marketing programs and rethinking how best to position their advancement areas to face future challenges. Many structures and approaches to implementation are emerging, and no one model will apply everywhere. Indeed, each institution's history, cultural values, management style, and leadership preferences will dictate final results. Still, because many basic assessment and planning processes are similar, the University of New Brunswick represents an excellent example.

A CLEARER PICTURE
The University of New Brunswick solved its marketing puzzle by improving its reputation and building a stronger brand
By Susan Mesheau

"Are you ready for this challenge?" That was the headline of the ad seeking a director of student recruitment and integrated marketing at the University of New Brunswick in Fredericton that piqued my interest.

The ad indicated that the institution, one of the oldest public universities in North America, had decided to take integrated marketing seriously. With a new mandate to build a stronger reputation and identity for UNB, senior administrators created a new position reporting directly to the president and a new office devoted to developing and marketing a consistent and focused brand.

Ah, I thought, a university that recognizes the power of marketing—and has commitment from the top and the impetus to do something about it. I was ready for that challenge, and in January 2001 I became that director. In September 2002, my colleagues and I launched UNB's first multiyear, fully integrated marketing program to create recognition and awareness of UNB.

We used a four-phase, market research-driven process based on these tenets: UNB must remain a national caliber institution; the university is critical to the economic, social, and cultural prosperity of the province and its people; and it needs more resources from government, business, alumni, and friends.

PHASE ONE: GETTING STARTED

A colleague of mine says integrated marketing is a way of thinking strategically, not to commercialize an institution but to make it known for its inherent value, build its reputation, and make it continually competitive in the marketplace. It's also about establishing institutional processes that mobilize people, get them on the same page, and move the institution forward. I'd add that it is built on the understanding and use of a very specific methodology. Marketing isn't really as sexy as folks think. It's mostly grunt work, starting with establishing top-level control through a champion, then gathering and analyzing market data, crafting solid plans and creative initiatives based on that data, generating university-wide buy-in and ongoing collaboration and communication, and last but certainly not least, measuring results.

With these thoughts in mind, I started from scratch. I spent my first three months at UNB solely focused on conducting a situational analysis that included an informal communications audit reviewing markets, audiences, needs, and communications materials. I discovered that the university had as many looks as it had publications; there was no main message and no compelling or focused brand. The university needed a strong foundation for its image- and brand-building efforts, something that would truly demonstrate the strength of its connection to the community, the province, the country, and alumni and prospective students.

Next, with the help of the UNB advancement director, who was the driving force behind the creation of the integrated marketing office and highly respected by the university community, I implemented an internal working infrastructure. We assembled a marketing committee made up of other advancement directors from UNB's two campuses to support the development and adoption of a UNB brand, the initial integrated marketing program, and all future marketing initiatives. We also assembled key stakeholder groups, including other university administrators, deans, directors, and students, to act as reporting and input audiences. We conducted quantitative and qualitative market research to set performance benchmarks, help us understand our perceived strengths and weaknesses, and test brand positioning and character words and phrases.

We also hired a marketing firm, M5 Communications, to assist in the development and implementation of our integrated marketing program. With the firm's help, the committee developed the main goals of UNB's image-building initiative: to create a cohesive brand image, to demonstrate to the people of New Brunswick how UNB is important to their daily lives, and to make them more predisposed to support the university in a variety of ways. We also needed to foster pride among alumni and internal constituents—faculty, staff, and students—and to mobilize them to advocate on UNB's behalf.

Initial market research found that awareness of UNB was high, but specific knowledge was lacking. Further, perceptions of the institution were neutral to positive, but people in the province did not see the university as connected to their lives. The research indicated that our audience considered jobs, health care, education, research, technology, and the environment important to their daily lives. We realized we could leverage UNB's strengths in these areas in our brand communications to create a halo effect over the entire university. Not a bad starting point.

PHASE TWO: STRATEGY DEVELOPMENT AND TESTING

We developed an initial program strategy that outlined target audiences (internal and external), our creative approach, key messages, slogan, and preliminary tactics. It took a long time to gain consensus, but we eventually created a family of cohesive "looks" that we would use on all UNB communications—a main corporate look for multicampus initiatives and individual but related looks for the two campuses.

In the past, UNB attempted to tell all of its stories all the time to every audience. We needed to determine our most powerful messages, better connect a particular audience's interests with UNB's strengths in those areas, and find inspired ways to communicate those strengths. In our advertising, we decided to use the real stories of UNB graduates, faculty, and staff members who are improving the quality of life of people in New Brunswick in the areas our audience told us were important. For example, 75 percent of educators in the province are UNB graduates, 70 percent of our nursing graduates practice in the province, 80 percent of the province's university research is conducted at UNB, and 28,000 UNB graduates live, work, and create jobs in the province. We used this information and compelling visuals to demonstrate how UNB is connected to the economic, social, and cultural prosperity of New Brunswick. Those messages, coupled with the campus brand looks, provided a standard foundation for all marketing efforts.

We then tested this planning and creative work by conducting interviews with stakeholder groups. At the same time, we tested several slogans with internal and external audiences before choosing Making a Significant Difference, which became the slogan for all university communications.

PHASE THREE: FINISHING TOUCHES AND IMPLEMENTATION

After extensive focus group testing, the committee finished the creative program and strategic plan. Image-building tactics included television and print ads and a new Web site. Relationship-building efforts included sending general information kits to stakeholders and the general public; hosting a tour around the province for the president to meet with alumni and government, business, and media representatives; sending regular, targeted e-mails to key audiences and internal communications about the awareness-building program and its results; and establishing a UNB spokespersons group, which provides advocacy support.

Because one of the main goals at the outset of this endeavor was to generate pride in and around UNB, we developed a special component of the plan aimed at UNB alumni, titled Proudly UNB, with its own complementary initiatives. Building on the same themes of how connected UNB is to the New Brunswick community and using the same look, we sent electronic newsletters and e-mails to alumni, placed ads in the alumni magazine that were similar to those we were running in major media outlets, provided postcards for alumni to send to the provincial government in support of the university, and mailed information kits to alumni about our efforts.

Because successful integrated marketing relies on mobilizing the entire university community, we conducted pre-launch information sessions about our image-building campaign—its rationale, plan, and benefits—and held a well-attended public and media marketing launch event concurrently on both campuses. These activities helped ensure public awareness and buy-in for what was essentially a new approach to university marketing.

PHASE FOUR: EVALUATION

Like initial market research and testing, formal post-implementation measurement is a critical component of an integrated marketing plan and too often is overlooked. So we made sure to devote time and effort to assessing the effectiveness of our efforts. After the first full year of the Making a Significant Difference effort, M5 Communications conducted an extensive quantitative survey with our audiences to compare awareness and current perceptions of UNB against benchmark data collected before the initiative started. The program exceeded first-year expectations. Perception of UNB measurably increased with the public and particularly with alumni. Seventy percent of all respondents—and 90 percent of alumni surveyed—could recall the ads, where they saw them, and what the ads said without being prompted. Seventy-one percent of respondents said UNB is relevant to New Brunswickers, and 66 percent felt it made a difference in their lives. The program had a number of other positive indirect outcomes, including a government funding increase from 6 percent to 10 percent of UNB's budget and a 4 percent increase in first-time donors. We also saw a 2 percent increase in active alumni involvement, a 6 percent increase in student enrollment, and an overall increase in regional and national media attention for UNB.

The program also caught the attention of our peers, earning a CASE Circle of Excellence Gold medal.

AN EVOLUTION IN PROGRESS

Adoption of UNB's new brand continues to grow internally and externally, and the effectiveness of the program is generating a new momentum and attitude at UNB. More people on campus want to become part of the program. Department staffers are requesting our assistance in using the graphic design guidelines—they want to use the new look so that their communications reflect the program.

As a result of our early accomplishments, we've developed an evolved Making a Significant Difference initiative, which builds on the success of the first year and reinforces the university's continued commitment to integrated marketing. We're now planning for year 3 of this program, and we have used this methodology and foundation to launch several other programs, including student recruitment, and to develop marketing initiatives to increase awareness of UNB research and UNB's College of Extended Learning. This program also has helped us position the president and the institution as leaders in the economic revitalization of our province. It's been an exciting, rewarding challenge. What do our plans for the future entail? This much is certain: We'll continue to expand UNB's marketing efforts—and continue to make a significant difference.

Susan Mesheau is director of student recruitment and integrated marketing at the University of New Brunswick, Fredericton campus, a Canadian institution with 12,000 students.

Reprinted from the September 2004 issue of CURRENTS magazine.

RETHINKING ADVANCEMENT FOUNDATIONS OUTLINE FOR A PROFESSIONAL DEVELOPMENT MASTER CLASS

The premise for this book is that higher education is facing a sea change brought on for the most part by government cutbacks. These cutbacks are forcing institutions to rethink fund-raising initiatives, tuition pricing, reputation-building tactics, alumni relations expectations, student recruiting practices and locations, program development planning, and much more. These changes have brought all the advancement professions to the forefront of overall university planning and management. And because of the nature of the changes, rethinking these functions increasingly is influenced by the basic ideas of integrated marketing.

The foundation of this master class, therefore, is the basic subject matter and strategies of integrated marketing. It is the way of thinking that, I believe, will inform effective change in all the other areas. The course begins with a discussion of the changes we are facing and the factors that are driving them. Discussions then address traditional areas of advancement, as well as related areas such as admissions and athletics that must change as well.

The content of this book will help advancement managers and master class facilitators explain the following topics and then lead discussions.

PART ONE: A CHANGING WORLD
1. **If the cold war is over, where is the global village?**
    Understanding was expected to improve
    Instead, more polarization
    Fueled by religion and politics
    Made worse by the news media

2. **The marketplace for higher education is changing, too.**
    Government cutbacks when we need higher education the most
    Searching for new sources of money and dealing with donor fatigue
    Increased competition for students, especially good ones
    Consumers becoming more sophisticated
    Calls for more visibility and enhanced reputations

3. **A need for a new breed of leader**
    For the world
    For institutions
    For advancement

4. **Characteristics of the new leader, for institutions and advancement**
    Passion for the business
    Understands all aspects of new technology
    Inspired by creative people
    Tolerance for ambiguity
    Wants to make a difference
    Wants leadership to know the latest thinking about organizations
    Focuses on the positive, what's working
    Generates aura of accessibility
    Admits mistakes, moves quickly beyond them
    Has a feel for managing process
    Likes institutional politics, manages conflict well
    Conveys self confidence
    Seeks productive partnerships
    Sees marketing as a way of thinking

5. **International issues and trends**
    Many common issues, beginning with cutbacks
    Competition, pricing, new markets, visibility, all shared needs
    A changing international student market, moving toward Asia

PART TWO: A NEW WAY OF THINKING THAT WILL INFLUENCE ALL
OF ADVANCEMENT

1. **Adapting marketing thinking to the academy**
   An adventure in ideas
   A way of thinking
   Making the total institution responsive to changing needs

2. **Key concepts**
   Creative teams
   Integration
   Relationships
   Dynamic leadership

3. **How integrated marketing works in the academy**
   Mobilizes talent, resources, and leadership
   Coordinates decentralized units
   Gets everyone on the same page
   Sees relationships as competitive advantage
   Focuses on overall institutional goals

4. **Sees basic principles of marketing underlying all planning and management**
   Products—both programs and the institution overall
   Price—cost versus perceived value
   Place—spaces, technology, college experiences
   Promotion—integration in a new media world
   Segmentation—meets audience needs but exceeds them
   Positioning—shaping competitive advantage, becoming best of breed
   Quality—broader standards, including product delivery

5. **Integrated marketing communication**
   Focuses on relationship building
   Prefers direct and interactive
   Targets stakeholders and opinion leaders
   Designs total-impact communication plans

6. **Dealing with changing news media**
   News business realities, 24/7 news/entertainment

Reputation-defining stories
A new office of communications
An internal agency approach
Account executive system
Visibility at what cost
Stakeholders and opinion leaders
Strategic special events
Image: "There are exciting things going on out there!"

7. **Affordable research**
By segment
Part of interactive communication
Only data that will inform decisions
Audits—profiles and benchmarking
Image surveys—awareness, attitude, and knowledge
Retention, customer satisfaction
Pricing elasticity
Media preference
Methods—direct mail, telephone surveys, interviews, focus groups, e-surveys,
   behavior observation

8. **Defining the brand**
Name visibility equals quality?
What is a brand? A feeling. A trust. A promise.
Message associated with a look
Repeated over and over
Message-on-a-page

9. **Building brand**
Clarify mission, vision, and values
Write a competitive advantage-defining sentence
List the specific features/benefits that best define your competitive advantage
List the facts that prove their truth
Identify the symbols and design characteristics that can be visual metaphors
   for your institution

10. **Developing sub-brands**
    Programs that can claim a distinct market
    85 percent sub-brand content; 15 percent overall university content

11. **When to use advertising**
    To have presence in a remote place
    To complement other tactics in a campaign
    Must saturate to be effective
    Can waste money, never one-time, never in response to a call

12. **Auditing operations**
    Develop an assessment question for each audit topic
    Conduct individual and small-group interviews with staff and executives
    Produce report that identifies strengths and weaknesses and makes suggestions
        for improved results

13. **Audit topics**
    Mission, vision, and values
    Current messaging
    Goals
    Media relations
    Internal communications
    Undergraduate admissions
    Special events
    Alumni relations communications
    Adult programs
    Organizational structure
    Executive attitudes
    Graphics standards
    Integration processes
    Issues management
    Internal marketing
    Fund-raising communications
    Advertising
    Athletics marketing
    Budgeting
    Management communications

Teamwork
Marketing research
Market segmentation
Crisis communication
Community relations
Publications
Web site
Graduate student recruiting
Personnel
Academic attitudes

14. **Audit follow-up**
Brief leadership and other participants
Recommend needed research
Fine-tune branding statement, message-on-a-page
Offer professional development master classes
Train task force
Write and implement special initiatives plan

15. **Effective action planning**
Blueprint outline (see Appendix B)
Mission, vision, and values
Institutional goals
Branding message and design guidelines
Initiatives for each priority market segment
Who will do what by when?

PART THREE: IMPLEMENTATION DISCUSSIONS

1. **Finding a peg for launching initiatives**
   An anticipated enrollment problem
   Preparing for a fund-raising campaign
   A revitalization initiative
   A new administration
   An outcome of strategic planning
   Criticism about visibility
   Recovering from a crisis
   Need to address a changing society

2. **Organizing to address changing needs**
   The role of leadership
   Reorganize?
   Form a task force?
   Taking organizational history and culture into account

3. **Finding a champion**
   Understands the changing society
   Understands marketing as a broad way of thinking
   Can explain all this to the academy
   Has credibility with academics
   Uses group process effectively
   Is determined to succeed and will persist

4. **Using process strategies and tactics**
   A university-wide marketing task force
   Action teams for special initiatives
   Editorial priorities group to find reputation-defining stories
   Account executives to help units develop comprehensive advancement plans
   Operations/marketing and communication/management group composed of
       central office unit heads

5. **Overcoming the barriers**

   Misunderstandings of what marketing is all about

   Threatened line managers

   Some have other priorities

   Work with those who get it

6. **Internal marketing**

   As opposed to internal communication

   Spreading the mission and brand

   "Getting on the same page" meetings

   Messages in the environment

   New faculty and staff orientation

   Human relations workshops on service

7. **Impact on fund raising**

   Dealing with donor fatigue

   Broadening the base

   Participatory approaches to building the case

   Involvement in the life of the university

   Cultivation by interest

   Use of technology

   Integrated communications packages

8. **Impact on alumni relations**

   Making the most of the alumni base

   Fund raising, student recruiting, and reputation building

   Lifecycle marketing

   Use of technology

   Use of word-of-mouth

   Cultivation by interest

   Career updating

   Educational enrichment

   Career counseling

9. **Impact on athletics**
    Making athletics make sense
    Integrating the operations
    Athletics marketing and the university
    University marketing and athletics

10. **Impact on student recruiting**
    Coming more under advancement
    Organizational change, or dotted line
    Differentiating, finding competitive advantage
    Auditing materials and communications
    Adding intensity and interaction
    Liking the students you have, finding more like them
    Creative segmentation
    Opening new markets: be careful
    Getting considered, closing the sale
    Adding initiatives on top of daily operations

11. **Advancement leadership**
    Thinks in big-picture terms and outside boxes
    Understands overall power of brand building
    Sees the integration of units
    Sees the world as target segments
    Bases decisions on research and analysis
    Sees crises and brand-building opportunities
    Wants to define the institution so that being the best in the world is possible
    Values internal and employee communication
    Uses process management effectively
    Sees why strategic planning must be market-driven
    Is personally driven and can successfully integrate life and work

SELECTED BIBLIOGRAPHY

Albrighton, Frank and Julia Thomas, Eds. *Managing External Relations*. Open University Press, 2001.

Beckwith, Harry. *The Invisible Touch: The Four Keys to Modern Marketing*. Warner Books, 2000.

Beckwith, Harry. *Selling the Invisible: A Field Guide to Modern Marketing*. Warner Books, 1997.

Beckwith, Harry. *What Clients Love: A Field Guide to Growing Your Business*. Warner Books, 2003.

Buchanan, Peter McE., Ed. *Handbook of Institutional Advancement*, 3rd ed. Council for Advancement and Support of Education, 2000.

Collins, Jim. *Good to Great: Why Some Companies Make the Leap...and Others Don't*. HarperCollins, 2001.

D'Alessandro, David F. *Brand Warfare: 10 Rules for Building the Killer Brand*. McGraw-Hill, 2002.

Friedman, Thomas L. *The World is Flat: A Brief History of the Twenty-First Century*. Farrar, Straus and Giroux, 2005.

Hayes, Thomas J. *New Strategies in Higher Education Marketing*. Haworth Press, 1991.

Innis, H.A. *The Bias of Communication*. University of Toronto Press, 1991.

Kirp, David L. *Shakespeare, Einstein, and the Bottom Line: The Marketing of Higher Education.* Harvard University Press, 2003.

Kotter, John P. *Leading Change.* Harvard Business School Press, 1996.

Lauer, Larry D. *Competing for Students, Money, and Reputation: Marketing the Academy in the 21st Century.* Council for Advancement and Support of Education, 2002.

Lauer, Larry D. *Communication Power: Energizing Your Nonprofit Organization.* Jones & Bartlett, 1997.

Lencioni, Patrick. *The Five Dysfunctions of a Team: A Leadership Fable.* Jossey-Bass, 2002.

Light, Richard L. *Making the Most of College: Students Speak Their Minds.* Harvard University Press, 2001.

McLuhan, Marshall. *Understanding Media: The Extensions of Man.* McGraw-Hill, 1966.

McKenna, Regis. *Relationship Marketing: Successful Strategies for the Age of the Customer.* Addison-Wesley, 1991.

Murphy, Mary Kay and Paul T. Smith. *Corporate and Foundation Support: Strategies for Funding Education in the 21st Century.* Council for Advancement and Support of Education, 2000.

"The Power of Design." *Fast Company,* June 2005.

Ries, Al and Laura Ries. *The 11 Immutable Laws of Internet Branding.* HarperCollins, 2000.

Ries, Al and Laura Ries. *The Fall of Advertising and the Rise of PR.* HarperCollins, 2002.

Ries, Al and Jack Trout. *Positioning: The Battle for Your Mind.* McGraw-Hill Professional Publishing, 2000.

Sevier, Robert A. *Integrated Marketing for Colleges, Universities, and Schools.* Council for Advancement and Support of Education, 1998.

Sevier, Robert A. *An Integrated Marketing Workbook for Colleges and Universities: A Step-by-Step Planning Guide.* Strategy Publishing, 2003.

Sevier, Robert A. *Building a Brand that Matters: Helping Colleges and Universities Capitalize on the Four Essential Elements of a Block-Buster Brand.* Strategy Publishing, 2002.

Larry D. Lauer is vice chancellor for marketing and communication at TCU (Texas Christian University) in Fort Worth, Texas, and an executive in residence in integrated marketing communication in the graduate program at the Schieffer School of Journalism. He directed the Commission on the Future of TCU, the institution's strategic planning project, in 2000.

Larry was founding chairman of the CASE Advanced Seminar on Integrated Marketing, a chair and faculty member of the CASE Summer Institute on Communication and Marketing at Duke and Vanderbilt Universities, as well as chair of the 2006 CASE Assembly in New York, A Summit on the Future of Higher Education and Advancement. He is the author of *Communication Power* (Jones & Bartlett, 1977), *Competing for Students, Money and Reputation: Marketing the Academy in the 21st Century* (CASE, 2002), and more than 25 journal articles and book chapters on integrated marketing and communication. He edited the section on marketing in the *Handbook of Institutional Advancement, 3rd edition* (CASE, 2000), where he is referred to as "pioneer of integrated marketing for our profession."

He received CASE's 2003 Alice L. Beeman Award for Research in Communication, the President's Award from Independent Colleges and Universities of Texas (ICUT) in 2003, and the Distinguished Achievement Award from CASE District IV in 2004. He has worked with more than 35 campuses in the U.S., Canada, South America, South Africa, the Caribbean, Australia, the United Kingdom, Europe and Singapore on integrated marketing initiatives, and has presented papers at countless regional, national and international conferences.

INDEX